LEADERSHIP
UNDER
pressure

PRAISE FOR *LEADERSHIP UNDER PRESSURE*

For me it was fascinating to see how the three circles model and the functional approach that I introduced at Sandhurst all those years ago served as a foundation for such an impressive story of excellent military leadership. What I particularly liked about it is the plain and unselfconscious insights it gives us into how a good leader can learn and grow by reflecting upon practical experience in the light of the abiding principles of leadership. The author strikes just the right balance between self-confidence and humility – being willing to go on learning about leadership throughout one's career. The balance is also I think just right between story-telling and teaching. The bridging between the military and the business world is another asset. I look on it as a real contribution to the field of leadership studies.

John Adair, leadership thinker, best-selling author and
United Nations Chair of Strategic Leadership

LEADERSHIP UNDER pressure

Tactics from the front line

COLONEL BOB STEWART

KOGAN
PAGE

London and Philadelphia

First published in Great Britain and the United States in 2009 by Kogan Page Limited

120 Pentonville Road
London N1 9JN
United Kingdom
www.koganpage.com

525 South 4th Street, #241
Philadelphia PA 19147
USA

© Colonel Bob Stewart, 2009

The right of Colonel Bob Stewart to be identified as the author of this work has been asserted by him in accordance with the Copyright, Designs and Patents Act 1988.

ISBN 978 0 7494 5655 9

British Library Cataloguing-in-Publication Data

A CIP record for this book is available from the British Library.

Library of Congress Cataloging-in-Publication Data

Stewart, Bob, Colonel.
    Leadership under pressure : tactics from the front line / Bob Stewart.
        p. cm.
    Includes index.
    ISBN 978-0-7494-5655-9
    1. Leadership. I. Title.
    HD57.7.S738 2009
    658.4'092—dc22

                                                                        2009017477

Typeset by JS Typesetting Ltd, Porthcawl, Mid Glamorgan
Printed and bound in India by Replika Press Pvt Ltd

Leadership is a universal skill throughout society. It is not necessarily overt, dominating or loud but very often exercised in a calm, thoughtful and even somewhat private manner. There are great many people who just lead in their own quiet way and to the very best of their ability, achieving great success as a result. But the best leaders always possess two common qualities: a passion and determination to succeed. With such thoughts in mind I dedicate this book to them and particularly:

Mr Chris McGrath
Headmaster of Donhead Preparatory School in Wimbledon

Whilst this book is my own work several friends were kind enough to read it and make comments; I'd like to thank Paul Skelton-Stroud, Ian Page, Simon Pearce and Jeremy Hein for their help.

Bob Stewart

Contents

About the author

Educated at Chigwell School, RMA Sandhurst, the University of Wales (1st, International Politics) and two military staff colleges, Bob Stewart completed 28 years in the Army. During that time he was awarded a Commendation in Northern Ireland for being the incident commander at the Ballykelly Bomb on 6th December 1982 and, in 1993, the DSO for gallantry and leadership whilst commanding his Battle Group under United Nations Command in Bosnia.

He left the Army as a Colonel in 1995 and first completed three years as Senior Consultant Public Affairs with Hill and Knowlton (UK) Ltd. Thereafter he became Managing Director of WorldSpace (UK) Ltd – a digital satellite broadcasting company. Since 2001 he has been an independent consultant specializing in political and security matters.

He writes for various national newspapers on political/security matters and is a regular commentator on radio and television. Stewart has written and presented a BBC World TV programme on leadership and a series of one-hour documentaries called *The Negotiator* for Channel 5 Television.

He is married and lives in Kingston-Upon-Thames.

Foreword

At the school I attended a long time ago, various soldiers, churchmen, diplomats and civil servants would come through from time to time and try to interest us in their chosen professions. There was even a representative of the colonial service (it was a *very* long time ago). They were all unanimous on one point. They assured us that we in our turn would be leaders of men. I would rather have been a leader of women, but women in those days did not get so much of a mention.

Then I got out into the real world, starting with a stint in the Army, and discovered that no one wanted to be led – at least by me. The highest rank that I reached in two years of undistinguished soldiering was that of acting sergeant.

People did, however, want to be led by Colonel Bob Stewart. For six months in Bosnia he was the British Army's most prominent field commander. His leadership was inspirational in difficult circumstances – a side war between Moslems and Croats with his Cheshire Regiment caught in the middle and having to improvise on its ambiguous UN mandate. He led by example, by precept, by common sense and force of personality. Luck also played a part. It always does.

This is a book about more than Bosnia and more than military matters. It analyses with style and insight the principles of leadership that apply as much in business and even politics as on the field of battle. Bob Stewart uses examples from his own career – for instance in dealing with adversity in Northern Ireland. He quotes widely from other authorities, soldiers as popular as General Slim and as abrasive as General Montgomery, to draw together a coherent account of what leadership is and what it isn't. It isn't telling people what to do. It is working with them, respecting them and inspiring them to work together to achieve a common objective.

The timing of this book is serendipitous. As an ex-politician as well as an ex-soldier, I believe that some of the lessons of *Leadership under Pressure* could be usefully absorbed and applied, at a time of acute political crisis, by politicians who have lost the people's trust.

One of Bob Stewart's principles is that the leader says what he is going to do and then goes out and does it. No spin and no dissimulation. It is an idea whose time has come.

Martin Bell OBE
Former BBC War Correspondent

Introduction

Ten good soldiers wisely led will beat a hundred without a head

Euripides, Greek Poet (480–406 BC)

6 APRIL 1993: CENTRAL BOSNIA

At just after 5 am a telephone ring woke me. As I stirred I heard huge explosions close together; incoming artillery fire? Quickly pulling the phone to my ear, I recognized the voice at the far end.

'Bob, is that you?'

'Yes, I'm here Bryan.'

'Do you know what's going on? The whole place has erupted. It's gone crazy. We're stuck in the middle of a major battle. You're miles away, on the wrong side of the lines', said Major Bryan Watters, my second in command.

The battalion operations room at Vitez was actually only some 20 miles from me as the crow flies, but it could only be reached by scaling a seriously large mountain on a winding, icy road. Last night I'd decided to stay in Zenica because the European Community ambassador had suggested we ate together. Afterwards it was late. If I remained in his hotel at least it would save me going back and then returning early the next day. We were both involved with intensive negotiations to recover a high-ranking Croat hostage from a mujahideen group. I was exhausted and stopping where I was avoided at least two hours of travelling, so I had sent my escort back to Vitez. They were told to come back for me in the morning. That decision was a big mistake. I was on my own and not where I should have been.

Just after first light, at about 7 am, I drove through Zenica and then turned up the mountain road. My route took me through three seemingly deserted checkpoints that required me to move both the barriers themselves as well as several protective mines. Twice I heard shots, possibly aimed at my Land Rover, and I could see shells landing on the surrounding slopes. Between checkpoints I drove as fast as the frozen, twisting pass would allow. Several times I saw dead bodies outside the smouldering remains of houses. The noise of battle was intense, particularly to the west.

After about 45 minutes a fourth checkpoint at Dubravica swung into view. I thanked God that two Warriors were positioned right behind it, their 30mm cannons obviously covering the Bosnian Croat soldiers at the checkpoint. A tall figure jumped out of the first Warrior. It was Sergeant Major 'Tiny' Lawson, gunner on my command Warrior. I drove forward and the Bosnian Croats opened the checkpoint – urged on without pleasantries by the sergeant major. 'Good morning Sergeant Major,' I said with great relief.

I was back where I should have been in the first place. My job was to command the British battalion group in Bosnia and that morning I had been in the wrong place, at the wrong time and with the wrong people.

Over the years I have led in many situations, often under considerable pressure. I have learnt something from experience and practice, even if I still make errors. But even the greatest leaders in history have made mistakes.

THE NEEDS OF LEADERSHIP

My first taste of what leadership was all about came when I was an officer cadet at the Royal Military Academy Sandhurst from 1967–69. At Sandhurst it was the leadership expert John Adair who introduced me to the idea that, in order to lead properly, officers had to understand three separate but interrelated needs:

- Task – the need to achieve a task, which is obviously the catalyst for action.
- Team – the need for people to work together as a team. Clearly many tasks necessitate collaboration with others.

- Individual – the needs of each individual in a team. Every person is unique and has differing requirements and priorities.

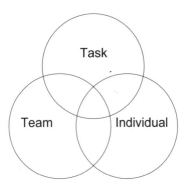

Figure 0.1 The needs of leadership
Source: © John Adair, *Training for Leadership* (1968)

John Adair's approach was fundamental to the way I was taught leadership and I am in his debt. It gets to the very roots of leading. But I will not go into more detail about these three needs here because anyone who wishes to know more can read any of the many books John has written to see it done properly. For my part I want to examine a direct spin-off from the needs of leadership – the functional and practical skills required by working leaders.

PRACTICAL LEADERSHIP UNDER PRESSURE

Leading is a multi-faceted skill; both a science and an art. It requires a hands-on approach, which is the theme of this book. I want to look at where we all come from as leaders, some decision-making tools that might help us and then examine a series of practical functions that leaders have to perform, or at least understand. Each chapter that now follows aims to throw light on the very practical business of leading under pressure.

The roots of leadership

Leaders come in many shapes and sizes and I am convinced they can be made or improved by training. When faced by a huge challenge

which one of us is not daunted or frightened by the enormity of it?
What we decide to do and how we tackle it is largely determined by
our experiences.

Decision-making tools

The army's ten principles of war can be applied to business. I have
always used four decision-making tools on operations; mission analyses, threat assessments, estimates and the negotiation template.
Throughout the book I give examples of where I have used such tools
in the military and commerce.

Preparation

The act or process of preparing for leading makes obvious sense. After
their election United States presidents have over two months to get
themselves ready for what will probably be the greatest challenge of
their lives. Preparation for any leadership appointment normally includes reconnaissance visits, research and a lot of thinking.

Intelligence

Knowledge of the likely opposition is crucial for leaders who have to
run any organization – military or civilian. Intelligence activities aim
to give a complete picture of opponents or competitors so as to gain an
understanding of what they are likely to do. However, intelligence data
is unlikely to be served up on a plate. Proper and accurate intelligence
is invaluable, but getting it requires diligence and hard work.

Innovation

Leaders are meant to provide ideas or at least be catalysts for them.
They are there to make things happen, to originate and not just to
follow procedures without challenging them to see if the job can be
done in a better way. In Bosnia I encouraged all ranks to think whether
our procedures could be improved. Quite often really good suggestions
came from private soldiers. After all, they did the business so knew
what they could and could not do in the field.

Planning

Preparing a plan will not guarantee success but not having one could be disastrous. Leaders are not just meant to sit there and let events take their course. They are required to intervene and change matters for the better. A good plan also shows subordinates that their leaders really understand the business in hand. Decent plans not only add to confidence but impact on morale as well.

Maintenance of morale

Field Marshal Lord Slim defined morale as a state of mind:

> It is that intangible force which will move a whole group of men to give their last ounce to achieve something, without counting the cost to themselves; that makes them feel they are part of something greater than themselves.

If looking after the spirit of an organization isn't a requirement of leaders I don't know what is. A leader must motivate his or her team to do their job to the very best of their ability.

Personal style

Style matters a great deal. The best leaders definitely have charisma. Sometimes it is a very quiet appeal without the need to be noisy, up-front or in your face. Everyone is different and tackles the job of leading in their own way. I had six company commanders in Bosnia and obviously each was different. Yet their training and experiences were very similar. However, if I were to give each one what was essentially the same task, I could guarantee they would each complete the job in different and often very diverse ways.

Tasking

Nobody can do everything and so allocating tasks is a really important command responsibility. Proper delegation not only encourages subordinates but it trains them too. In the Balkans my responsibilities were so huge that I simply could not be everywhere or take charge of everything. A basic decision I made early in planning was that I needed to be in Bosnia with the very first, small advance elements. In consequence I decided that my second in command, still in Germany, would take responsibility for all training and thereafter deployment all the way into positions in Central Bosnia. Once positioned properly in Bosnia I put him charge of the operations room so that I was left free to locate myself wherever I felt it to be necessary.

Supervision

Leaders should be where they can have the maximum effect on those they lead. In his famous 1832 work *On War*, Carl von Clausewitz suggested leaders should be close to the 'Schwerpunkt' – the point of concentrated effort. In Bosnia I followed von Clausewitz's dictum almost religiously – moving to where I thought the most vital part of the battalion's operations were taking place. It was rare that I was at my operational headquarters for long because I wanted to be in a position to supervise or control from where the action was or at the very least a position from where I really could understand, first-hand, what was happening.

Courage and example

In a dynamic situation those in charge must be prepared to lead, if necessary with considerable courage and certainly by example. This encompasses both the physical side of action, such as being in the front lines, and providing an example in the way you work and deal with colleagues. Everyone understands that an injunction to 'Do what I do rather than what I say' is by the far best way to operate as the boss.

Negotiation

'Heads I win, tails you lose' is not negotiation. The best negotiation occurs when everyone involved feels they have gained something. It is poor negotiation if any side feels they have been short-changed or diddled, or have given away too much for whatever reason. The best negotiations are those whose results stand the test of time.

Communication

In the military world you sometimes have to communicate or die. In the business world you have no choice; you have to communicate or fail. Today leaders need to be able to reach all kinds of audiences. They have to speak to colleagues at every level. Naturally they have to talk with their customers as well. Then there are reporters, suppliers, distributors, investors, analysts, local communities, politicians and local authorities, regulatory authorities and more. Getting messages right – particularly when a crisis hits – is a crucial responsibility of business leaders.

Crisis management

Crises are unpredictable. The only predictability about them is that they will inevitably happen. Dealing satisfactorily with crises is where a leader really earns his or her money. In a crisis the leader matters more than almost anything else. Failure to react properly can have deadly results in the army, and commercially it might determine whether a company survives or not.

Reflections

I believe leading under pressure is probably the greatest challenge there is. In the final chapter I reflect on the issues in the book, and also spend a little time examining vital leadership qualities, including passion, self-belief, emotion, robustness, luck, prejudice and personal care.

THE JOY OF LEADING

So far I haven't mentioned the great thrill that comes from leading. Let me be absolutely clear on this. Leadership is not just a privilege but it can be great fun too – even under pressure. That sense of enjoyment should also trickle down to subordinates. Of course there are challenges, and sometimes you may feel great fear, but being the boss should be something that gives great personal joy. And that enjoyment can also be a superb stress buster too.

As my battalion drove out of Bosnia at the end of our time there, I stopped on a ridge overlooking the huge plateau stretching below me. I could see for miles and watched company columns of armoured vehicles as they drove south towards the Croatian border. They had spread out right across the plateau and did not constrain themselves to tracks. From my position I could see almost every tracked vehicle in my battalion. They looked like a swarm of white ants crawling across the countryside. I was thrilled by the sight. There were my soldiers, we had done our job to the best of our ability and I was taking almost all of them home when we had anticipated losing far more people. I was immensely pleased with our achievements. It was a fantastic feeling. What an honour it had been to command such people, who had done so much good despite the vicious battles in which we had been involved. As I watched well over a hundred vehicle dust trails in the distance I experienced the greatest professional joy of my life.

SELECT A LA CARTE

We are all the product of our experiences. What happened to me has shaped how and what I think, how I behave and the way I believe those in charge should function. There is no definitive or exact way to lead, and what I write about in this book is my own personal view. I am no academic, so forgive me if I do not really care too much about the precise differences between, say, mission and vision, or mission command and empowerment. I have tried instead to make this book about practical leadership – especially leadership under pressure.

Every one of us is different and we all tackle our own particular situation in our own way. Please do not think I am suggesting a rigorous approach that must be strictly adhered to. People can decide for themselves whether to follow my ideas. All I have tried to do is to outline what I think and how I tackled leading in my own imperfect way. Some of what I say will not be appropriate for everyone or every situation, so please highlight what you think is apposite à la carte.

1

The roots of leadership

A leader has got to learn to dominate the events which surround him; he must never allow these events to get the better of him; he must allow nothing to divert him from his aim; he must always be on top of his job, and be prepared to accept responsibility.

Field Marshal Viscount Montgomery of Alamein in
Military Leadership

LEADERSHIP: NATURAL AND ACQUIRED

There are some people who have innate leadership qualities from birth. Why this happens is a mystery but it does. I have seen such individuals throughout my life. Some lucky folk just have natural confidence, which they can utilize to influence others around them whatever is happening. This is sometimes apparent at a very young age.

I have six children and over the years, as I have watched them playing with friends, it has become obvious to me that some kids are more assertive and confident than others. They may also be more positive and up-front with adults. Often they are the ones who are also keen to try something first. I suspect these children are natural leaders – at least for their age.

Whether leadership traits in children continue into adulthood is by no means guaranteed but in my experience they often do. Confident children normally become self-assured adults. So the question must be whether less outgoing youngsters can be converted into good leaders by the appropriate training. The answer is most definitely yes.

I was not a born leader. As a boy I was very timid. My younger brother, Andrew, who later grew up to command 201 Squadron RAF, was far more self-assured than me. Indeed, when we were away at prep school, I remember that frequently he would fight my battles. Throughout my schooldays I knew in my heart that I was much more a follower than any kind of leader.

My deep love and respect for my father translated into a fervent wish to be an RAF officer like him. But at the age of 13 we discovered I was slightly red–green colour blind and could not therefore train as aircrew. I remember my father making light of it and suggesting that I could always join the Army, as they would take anyone! But I was very upset that I was unable to be like Dad. When I was 17 I applied for the Army, attending the Regular Commissions Board at Westbury on its four-day officer selection course. To my amazement I passed.

At the Royal Military Academy Sandhurst I concentrated very hard on just surviving the first few months of intensive training, which I found hard and exhausting. I felt sure that the Army would rumble that I just wasn't good enough. But I was still there after two terms when several of my friends had quit, been returned to their units or been thrown out.

Then something strange began to happen. The longer I survived at Sandhurst the more my confidence grew. When given testing or demanding leadership command tasks to complete I wasn't great but didn't seem to do too badly. The tipping point came for me when Colour Sergeant Roger Coleman, my instructor, told me that one day I 'might' make a good officer. His encouraging words had a dramatic effect on my self-confidence.

Sandhurst took me in as a shy, timid boy and during two years of training produced a much more confident specimen. I passed out from the Royal Military Academy sixth in its overall order of merit, with the Military History and English prizes. But deep down I still knew that I had a long way to go.

I joined the 1st Battalion the Cheshire Regiment in Bahrain the day after I graduated from Sandhurst. From then onwards I ploughed on, learning my trade as I progressed upwards from second lieutenant. Lots of training, operations and associated experiences with soldiers made leading easier.

Eight years later I returned to Sandhurst as a captain instructor. As part of my job I had to note who was and who wasn't a natural leader.

But I soon realised that both so-called born leaders, as well as those who had to work at it, improved their performances considerably with training and encouragement. By then I was convinced that everyone, no matter how senior, could benefit by learning or revising leadership skills.

21 AUGUST 1992

Being in charge is no soft option. Obviously it carries privileges like better pay, improved conditions and greater chances of advancement. But being the boss also includes much larger responsibilities and bigger challenges. For me the greatest responsibilities and principal challenges of my life to date started one day towards the end of August 1992 after I had been a lieutenant colonel in command of the Cheshires for 18 months.

I had been on leave at a hotel in Berlin for less than a day. It was lunchtime. The receptionist saw me and called me over. She handed me a phone saying the call was urgent. At the other end was Major Tim Park, my second in command, speaking from the battalion's base at Fallingbostel, 120 miles away in Lower Saxony.

'This afternoon they're going to announce we're sending a force to the Balkans,' he explained.

'Poor devils!' I replied.

'No, you don't get it. We're the force and you're being announced as our commander in a couple of hours!'

I froze in panic.

UNIVERSAL LEADERSHIP

I suspect many people must have also experienced that heart-stopping moment when presented with some totally new and unexpected challenge. What you do next and how you do it matter greatly. Above all, blind panic is obviously wrong and hugely counter-productive. Keeping calm is crucial. If the boss looks terrified and unsettled then that feeling spreads like wildfire.

Leadership principles are universal. They are no different whether you happen to be in the army or in business. Of course, business executives don't usually have to make life and death decisions, but the same is true for army officers – most of the time. Yet business leaders sometimes make choices that drastically affect peoples' lives – they hire and fire. In life and death terms they could be in charge when there is a major fire or perhaps a poisonous gas leak or even a slowly sinking ship when vital decisions may be required. During 1999 the satellite radio company I worked for insisted on sending two engineers into Macedonia to carry out field trials. Personally I thought this was not particularly wise. I said so but it wasn't my decision. At the time conditions there were hardly benign – especially on the roads. In the event one of the engineers was killed when his vehicle slid off a mountain in the wintry conditions. The executive who insisted the trials went ahead was severely affected and could not stop blaming himself.

STEREOTYPES

Given its operational history, the British Army should know a thing or two about leadership. It has been involved in military campaigns and life and death decisions long enough. Some people retain a stereotypical image of the Army, which they imagine to be filled with incompetent officers, screaming sergeant majors, brutal corporals and the rest. That is far from reality today.

The Army has a fairly enlightened view of leadership. The modern Army officer is normally the total reverse of the unthinking, unintelligent, uncaring upper-class nitwit as so often portrayed inaccurately in comedy films and television programmes. Real Army officers wouldn't last five minutes if they were like that.

Leaders make things happen. The reason why people are placed in charge is so that they can make choices that work and make circumstances better. If officers or business executives were to simply follow orders without question and execute a plan according to a set formula, the job could be done by anyone who passes by. What separates officers from soldiers, and business executives from other employees is the fact that both groups are deliberately positioned to determine strategy and then lead others.

I have met and talked with a great number of business executives since I left the Army in 1995. Many of them seemed excellent leaders, but what always surprised me was just how little time they have spent learning about or practising leadership skills. Some even told me they had had no leadership training whatsoever. In a way that is scandalous. As an officer cadet I probably spent about 60 per cent of my time directly learning how to lead.

Obviously a military officer takes superior orders and applies them practically. In the Army considerable autonomy is given to subordinate officers. Once individual missions or tasks are allocated, they take full personal responsibility and are normally allowed as much flexibility as possible to achieve them. The military term for this process is mission command.

MISSION COMMAND AND EMPOWERMENT

Mission command is a military technique that stresses decentralized command, freedom, speed of action and initiative. Understanding their leader's intentions, their own missions and the context of those missions, officers are told what effect they are to achieve and the reason why it needs to be achieved. It is then up to them to decide how best to achieve their own objectives.

Mission command has its equivalent in business. It's called empowerment. Defined as the process of increasing the capacity of individuals or groups to make their own choices and to transform those choices into desired actions and outcomes, empowering executives is quite normal these days. To me, mission command and empowerment seem interchangeable terms as both indicate firm intentions and give freedom to act.

Being empowered allows business leaders to make quick, advantage-taking decisions to achieve their ends. Their job is to make things work by making good personal decisions, hopefully with a touch of inspiration. They lead by reference to strategy, tactics, regulations and above all common sense, but they are given the power to challenge conventional wisdom too. The very best leaders are those whose thought processes are not ultimately constrained by regulations or reliance on doing it just how it has always been done. Some call this approach thinking outside the box. Empowered leaders adapt flexibly to new circumstances in order to succeed.

THE NEW BROOM

When anyone becomes a leader the old guard watch, waiting to see what impact on their lives the new broom may have. Sometimes a leadership change can have dramatic impact. In 1940 a private secretary noted the instant impact of Winston Churchill's arrival as Prime Minister:

The effects of Churchill's zeal were felt immediately in Whitehall. Government departments, which under Neville Chamberlain had continued to work at much the same speed as in peacetime, awoke to the realities of war. A sense of urgency was created in the course of very few days and respectable civil servants were actually to be seen running along the corridors. No delays were condoned; telephone switchboards quadrupled their efficiency; the Chiefs of Staff and the Joint Planning Staff were in almost constant session; regular office hours ceased to exist and weekends disappeared with them.

Leaders have to determine exactly how to play being in charge. A careful balance has to be struck. Excessive zeal might get that person branded a pain in the backside by both juniors and seniors alike. Alternatively an over-timid, too amenable approach can easily diminish the authority of leadership. I recall instances of new platoon commanders simply allowing their platoons to run themselves, making no personal impact whatsoever. It wasn't long before they were considered a piece of furniture. Shortly thereafter they were normally sacked or posted away.

First impressions matter. Early actions and decisions are vital in building a reputation so getting your initial approach right is very important. Better to be perceived as distant than too easy. Major Dick Peel, my first company commander, briefed me as a brand new second lieutenant that being too formal or strict initially can be corrected later, but being over-familiar or slack would be very difficult to sort out. It is for this reason that brand new officers are told to be absolutely proper and correct in at least their first few months. Use of first names and frequent boozy nights out with the boys simply asks for trouble. The old phrase 'familiarity breeds contempt' can certainly apply if a young officer, the same age as most of his soldiers, doesn't keep a certain distance from those to whom he may have to issue unpopular orders at some time. Once established as the boss such taboos might not be required, but it is always better to be safe than sorry.

DISTINCT ORGANIZATIONAL STYLES

Every organization, Army regiment or commercial company has its own ethos, style and ways of doing things. It is very important to get to know the way things are done and expected norms of behaviour. Usually Army regiments do this by keeping young officers 'under instruction' until they find their feet. There is a hierarchical structure and new officers getting it wrong are corrected, sometimes rather publicly, by their brother officers, company commanders, commanding officers and especially the regimental sergeant major, who can be terrifying to second lieutenants!

But in business it seems new executives are often left to find their own feet. They are sometimes expected to be fully up to speed from the moment they arrive, and receive very little guidance on company etiquette or how to behave. That seems wrong to me, and it must be counter-productive. I never received any formal induction training in the two big appointments of my business life and I certainly felt such training would have helped. Unless they are divine, everyone needs some familiarization training or help in a new role.

FEAR OF THE CHALLENGE

In the late summer of 1992 my battalion was an armoured infantry battalion consisting of about 750 soldiers equipped with Warrior armoured fighting vehicles. I was naturally excited, invigorated and somewhat overwhelmed on being told that I was to lead the battalion on what was sure to be a highly risky military operation in the Balkans. But I was also very apprehensive, because the chances of considerable casualties and overall failure seemed high.

I had watched the television news since the Balkan wars had started and the pictures I saw made me turn cold. My fears were fed by both the press and the Ministry of Defence (MoD) itself. Most newspapers, television and radio reports forecast disaster for any British deployment into what Churchill had called 'the Cockpit of Europe'. They suggested it was highly likely that thousands of people would die in our area from starvation, cold and a lack of medical supplies, regardless of what we did. The press hardly rated our chances. Then officers in the MoD's military operations branch worried me further. They bluntly told me that I should prepare for casualties as great as one in four.

Given a new and difficult task, many people get nervous and wonder whether they are up to it. Personally, I was frightened. There were two main reasons for this. First, I wasn't sure that I could carry it off – I had a lot of self-doubt. Second, I was very concerned about the possibility of heavy casualties. That had happened to me before. In

1982 six soldiers had been killed and over thirty wounded from my company whilst I had been serving in Northern Ireland. I still think about this loss daily. But I didn't really have time to ponder too much – I was the leader, and that job required me to sort out what was to happen.

BUILDING A SENSE OF DIRECTION

First I had to determine exactly what I was expected to achieve in the Balkans. The Army calls this the mission. A military mission translates into words like objective, aim or goal in business speak. I notice, though, that many business leaders are perfectly happy to use the word mission, even though this particular phrase has a definite military connotation. It is normal and standard operational procedure for military commanders to be given a clear mission as they start planning for action. But that didn't happen to me in 1992.

My first briefing in the MoD took place on a Sunday morning. Just before 10 am a contingent of senior officers and civil servants trooped into Historic Room 79, a large conference hall right in the middle of the Whitehall building. About 60 people were present but the briefing was aimed directly at me and another officer.

For an hour and a half we were briefed on the history of the Balkans. I expected some description of what we were to do there, but it never came. Nobody told me where I should be going or indeed what would be the mission. Without knowing what I was supposed to achieve planning was a little difficult, to say the least. Everything was very tentative. It was clear that most officers present had severe misgivings about the operation. Nonetheless, I was told to join a reconnaissance team and go to the Balkans to see for myself.

The main purpose of my reconnaissance was to find us a role in the United Nations Protection Force operation being established in Bosnia. The Army had been committed to action by political decision, apparently with very little military input or advice on what we might be able to do. It seemed our real purpose might be simply to assist the United Nations High Commission for Refugees (UNHCR) to deliver aid – nothing more. But nobody was sure of that either. Major General Rupert Smith, present at the briefing and until recently my own divisional commander in Germany, scrawled a note and passed it along the front row to me. Encouragingly it read: 'Bob, It looks like a "crock of sh*t"! Best of luck. Rupert.'

In fairness, though, the MoD was not in a position to give me either a clear idea of what it wanted to achieve or indeed of what my mission was on the ground, because the international politics of the whole endeavour were still being fixed. But that was no practical help to me. I was to be deployed into a conflict zone and we needed to have a clear mission to guide our actions. Soldiers must fully understand what is to happen and what they themselves must achieve.

In business I have seen similar situations where top leaders either give no specific aim to subordinates or cloud it mightily by wrapping all sort of requirements and conditions into their instructions. The truth is that every leader, military or civilian, requires a clearly understood, mission, objective, aim or goal from which they can plan. It should be brief, lucid and pertinent.

Seven years later, when I was out of the Army and a regional managing director of a multinational company, my parent company didn't once give me any aims, objectives or targets. I was amazed, because the only real instruction was simply to attain more (but more of what?) with fewer resources, and scant help or direction on how that might be achieved. Well-defined, clearly communicated goals are vital.

2

Decision-making tools

The general must know how to get his men their rations and every other kind of stores needed for war. He must have imagination to originate plans, practical sense and energy to carry them through. He must be observant, untiring, shrewd; kindly and cruel; simple and crafty; a watchman and a robber; lavish and miserly; generous and stingy; rash and conservative. All these and many other, natural and acquired, he must have. He should also, as a matter of course, know his tactics; for a disorderly mob is no more an army than a heap of building materials is a house.

Attributed to the Greek Philosopher Socrates (469–399 BC)

DOING THE RIGHT THING

Doing the right thing is sometimes very difficult. In 1936 George Orwell, the English author, published a famous essay about how he killed an elephant. Ten years before, in 1926, he had been a colonial policeman in Burma. Orwell had been called upon to deal with a normally tame elephant that had just killed a man. The elephant was enraged by coming into what is called 'musth', a condition where the testosterone of a bull elephant rises to up to 60 times its normal level and which often makes it almost uncontrollable. Armed with a large calibre rifle and followed by a crowd of 2,000 people expecting a good show, Orwell headed to the paddy fields where the elephant had stopped to graze.

By the time Orwell reached the elephant it had reverted to its normal docile state and he was reluctant to kill it. But the crowd fully expected him to do so and, because of that, Orwell believed he had little choice. He felt trapped by their expectations that a colonial administrator would act with determined ferocity. In consequence he felt he had to fire. Clumsily he shot the elephant time and time again before he left it dying in agony. Afterwards his colonial colleagues were divided in their opinion as to whether he acted correctly or not. But Orwell secretly pondered whether any of them ever understood that the real reason he fired was to avoid looking like a fool in front of a massive crowd. Orwell regretted killing that elephant for the rest of his life.

When I think about a leader's responsibility to do the right thing I always recall an incident that happened on my first operational tour in Northern Ireland. Second Lieutenant Harry Conlin had been a little senior to me at Sandhurst, joining the battalion some six months before me. But now we were both platoon commanders together on our first operational tour.

A few weeks after we had arrived in Northern Ireland Harry was ordered to take his platoon of 36 soldiers down to the town of Auchnacloy in South Tyrone, where he had been told that he had to back up the Royal Ulster Constabulary (RUC). There had been some rioting in the town and the RUC felt that a military presence might help. Harry drove to the RUC station but the police refused to come out. They had barricaded themselves inside. The RUC said a large crowd was building up in the town's centre and Harry was told by the police to deal with it alone. The platoon only had one vehicle, a four-ton truck, and so Harry had no chance to reconnoitre discreetly before he went into town.

Harry's platoon was keyed up. In the previous week they had been taunted as 'virgin soldiers' by their friends in other companies because they had been sent to Belfast and were away when the rest of the battalion were involved in riots in Londonderry. Now they thought they would be in a position to stifle the jeers of their colleagues.

The crowd immediately noticed the platoon's arrival, and people started chanting, jeering and throwing things. But Harry saw that the crowd was leaving a church hall and, whilst noisy and unfriendly, was actually not a riotous assembly equipped for battle. He felt the police had slightly over-reacted, perhaps by calling in the military in the first place and certainly by skulking inside their base station. In Harry's view his arrival had exacerbated the problem, so he made a decision. Departing rather than staying should calm matters and possibly avoid violence.

Figure 2.1 Harry Conlin instructing on the ranges

The platoon was hyped up and ready for the action that, so far in their operational tour, they had been denied. But Harry told them that he felt it would be better to leave, and ordered the soldiers back onto the truck. This almost caused a mutiny. Even Harry's platoon sergeant remonstrated with his young officer. However, Harry had made his mind up that this was the right decision, and that was that. He stuck to what he thought to be right. Harry and his platoon drove out of town, the crowd dispersed and all became peaceful again.

After this event his soldiers questioned his judgement almost to the extent of accusing him of cowardice, and their comments went as high as the commanding officer, who interviewed Harry the next day. Harry stuck to his guns, saying that what he had done was right. Somewhat reluctantly, the commanding officer accepted Harry's explanation. Nonetheless, Harry felt absolutely wretched and even contemplated leaving the Army. His decision was right and proper, even if his soldiers could not see it. It took him some time after that to regain his reputation as a first-class platoon commander with just as much courage as any other.

I recall the incident well because it seemed to me that Harry's decision, unpopular as it was, demonstrated true grit and leadership. It was a very good example of the loneliness of command at a very young age. Harry knew his job was to calm the situation, and he believed that it would best be achieved by withdrawing his troops. If Harry had committed his soldiers against the crowd he would have done so for much the same reason that George Orwell felt he had to kill the elephant. Harry thought he was right and Orwell thought he was wrong. Leading is about making the right decisions, even if they are unpopular, and Harry had most certainly done that. He had decided what needed to be done and stuck to it. In doing so Harry Conlin had obeyed the first principle of war.

THE PRINCIPLES OF WAR

The Army lists ten principles of war.

1. Selection and maintenance of the aim.
   Decide what you want to achieve and do all you can to get it.
2. Concentration of force.
   Engage the enemy's weakness with your strength.
3. Economy of effort.
   Do not waste precious resources.
4. Maintenance of morale.
   Keep spirits up in your team.
5. Offensive action.
   Maintain tempo by attacking your opponent.
6. Flexibility.
   Be prepared for the unexpected and deal with it.
7. Cooperation.
   Ensure that all components of a team work in unison to achieve the aim.
8. Security.
   Keep your secrets just that.
9. Surprise.
   Ensure your opposition knows nothing of your plans until it is too late.
10. Sustainability.
    Maintain your capability to operate.

Not one of these ten headings needs much of a re-write to make it applicable to business.

- Like Harry Conlin, every leader should start by deciding what needs to be achieved (1).
- Leaders will want to exploit competitors' weaknesses whilst maximizing their own strengths (2).
- Obviously resources are precious so they must be used well and to good effect (3).
- High morale or spirits translate directly into better productivity (4).
- Keep competitors on their mettle by making them worried about what you are doing (5).
- Expect the unexpected to happen and plan what you will do when it does (6).
- Make sure everyone understands what is required and works together as a team (7).
- If confidentiality is required, ensure you have the means to achieve it (8).
- Surprising your competitors is a great way to seize and keep the initiative (9).
- Finally, make sure you have enough finance and resources to achieve your aim (10).

TIMELINESS

Over 250 years ago a dutiful but somewhat dogmatic admiral was on the quarter-deck of his flagship arguing a point with his flag captain. As he did so the enemy French fleet was within striking distance and at his mercy. But the admiral was apparently too busy discussing at length whether the way he proposed to station his ships in the attack would be in strict accordance with rules and regulations laid down by the Admiralty. As he procrastinated, the French slipped away.

At the time British naval law insisted on a mandatory death penalty for any officer who did not do his utmost against the enemy either in battle or pursuit. Vice Admiral John Byng was arrested, tried by court martial and found guilty. He was shot on 14 March 1757 in the Solent on the forecastle of HMS *Monarch*. Byng's problem, sadly a deadly one, was that he could not make an effective decision in time.

Time is always of the essence and well thought through, opportune reactions to a problem stand the best chance of achieving an early resolution. Getting on with it is good advice. In 1835 the Duke of Wellington announced to Earl Stanhope, 'My rule was always to do the business of the day in the day.' Sir Stuart Rose, Chief Executive of Marks & Spencer, agrees:

> Don't do tomorrow what you could today. Quite often you know what you want to do, instinctively or through experience. Don't spend too long analysing and checking it when you should actually just get on with it. It doesn't matter what business you are in today, they are all so fast moving that time is advantage or money.

Dithering may lose competitive advantage and money, and procrastination can be a huge opportunity cost, but equally a decision made too quickly and on the wrong basis could bring disaster. Judging the right time for action is a leadership skill and the trick is to get the correct decision made at the right moment.

Yet decision makers rarely have all the relevant facts they would wish for when they feel they must act. At this point instinct, gut reaction and, most important of all, sheer luck probably take over. Once, when Napoleon was leading a selection process for promotion to general officer, he noted the courage, experience and professional proficiency of all the candidates but asked one further question: 'Yes, yes to all that but just tell me how lucky they are'.

FOUR DECISION-MAKING TOOLS

Almost unconsciously, all of us have a method of looking at problems that we use again and again, sometimes throughout our lives. We probably don't even realize this because we do it without thinking. Ninety-nine per cent of the routine choices we make each day are made without conscious thought. Do we think about the way we walk, put on shoes, open a door or make a drink? Most people don't notice such habitual decision-making. If you drive a car, think how often do you do so on some form of mental auto-pilot. Our minds don't even bother to consult us for so many choices – such as taking a breath or blinking. So why should we need help to make any decisions?

The answer is that we don't – at least for the 99 per cent of choices we make unconsciously or in our stride. But some decisions are different. These are not routine, by rote or unconscious. These require mindful selection. The most complex of them may even require extensive research, diligent analysis, careful evaluation of options and a judgement on the way forward. Most people, including myself, are grateful for any help they can get in these circumstances.

I use four specific decision-making tools when facing a difficult problem. I first employed them in the Army and continue to do so in commercial life:

Tool 1: Mission analysis
Tool 2: Threat assessment
Tool 3: Estimate
Tool 4: Negotiation

TOOL 1: MISSION ANALYSIS

Too often, it seems, people simply do not understand exactly what they have to do when given a task. The Army has a particular process, 'mission analysis', that will help people to examine the nature of a task and what it might involve. Mission analysis is a method of helping to determine what a given task really means. It involves a detailed investigation into the purposes and intentions behind what is to be planned.

Planning itself is often very boring – much better to take action. But a real understanding of exactly what you need to achieve is vitally important before doing anything. If you don't sort out what is really needed then you are likely to go off in the wrong direction and straight into likely failure.

Successful mission analysis helps in two ways. First, it ensures you understand your objective and comprehend fully in what way you personally contribute to overall strategy. Second, and most important, it should give you insight and guidance as to how you might achieve your aim.

Figure 2.2 Mission analysis

Mission analysis consists of three steps, considered in turn. The steps look simple enough but they can involve a tremendous amount of detailed research and work. I always use the process to get my thoughts in order. But I have never used mission analysis if I felt I needed to be a slave to it. To that end I try to make any mission analysis as short as possible – normally completing the process on one side of paper and in its three constituent parts.

1. Mission
   Mission Analysis should start immediately someone receives an objective from a superior, or perhaps to anticipate a new requirement. It is simply an examination of what the mission means. In reality missions are often a bit fuzzy or obscure – especially if they haven't been thought through by whoever issues them. I accept there may sometimes be a good reason for this but in such circumstances mission analysis is probably even more important. So the first step is to get a very clear idea of what you are being asked to do.
2. Tasks
   This is a check to help understand exactly what tasks are important in order to achieve the mission. For example, you may be given a mission to capture a hill but that could not be achieved unless, for instance, your forces had enough ammunition or were able to get into a position to assault the objective. In business, selling a new product line would only be possible if you had sufficient stock numbers and could get them into shops on time. Understanding exactly what tasks are required is vital to designing any plan.
3. Resources and constraints
   A review of resources and constraints is entirely logical. An understanding of exactly what resources you have available during operations determines what you can and cannot do. Constraints, of course, can be imposed from above or by other factors such as lack of resources, weather or geography.

Mission analysis working

I was formally warned that I would be commanding the task force for the Balkans at lunchtime on 21 August 1992. By 6.30 am the next day, having driven four hours from Berlin back to my base at Fallingbostel in North Germany, I produced my first mission analysis on the operation. Determining exactly what my battalion had to achieve was my crucial

first requirement. That mission analysis wasn't detailed but it contained
enough to help those below me start operational preparation. Leaders,
whether in the military or in business, must get information about what
is going to happen down to their subordinates as soon as possible. To
that end I arranged a conference for all officers at 10.30 am on 22
August to discuss and agree how we should prepare the battalion for
what was to come. Below I have reproduced an unclassified version of
that mission analysis.

Getting vital information out to those who are going to be involved
is a prime requirement. In that way people can start to prepare for

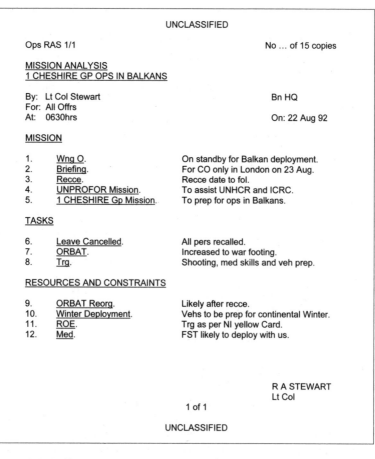

Figure 2.3 Balkan operation mission analysis

what is to happen, and preparation time is maximized. The Army calls this process concurrent activity; various levels in the team, having been warned off quickly, get on with their own particular preparations for an operation. People can thus maximize and make the best use of the time they have to sort themselves out. Even just a one-page summary giving as many facts as are known or surmised is valuable. When I have been in charge of an organization, I always felt that I had failed if someone said to me, 'Nobody tells me anything'. It is the duty of leaders to make sure that their staff or employees are informed about forthcoming changes as soon as possible.

In today's business environment few executives believe they ought to know everything – too much detail can cause confusion. Of course, they must know what will affect them, directly or indirectly, but they do not need to know every single detail of a complicated plan. It is probably better to have a broad understanding of what is happening and concentrate on what they need to know to do their particular job. Some people call this particular aspect of information 'relevant knowledge'. The Army teaches this 'relevant knowledge' approach as a decision-making technique.

Vision and mission

There is obviously a direct relationship between vision and mission. Business books define vision as a mental image of a future result. It is meant to be simple, clear and precise. Executives should refer to it all the time and it is meant to guide their strategy.

Both vision and mission are a leader's responsibility. He or she should provide that clear picture of the future and ensure that it meets the changing needs of the organization matched against the environment in which it operates. There are clear definitional differences between visions and missions. A mission defines an organization's purpose and primary objectives, whereas a vision also defines purpose in general but adds in the values of an organization. A mission concentrates more on how you operate whereas a vision also looks at why you should do so.

A vision thus overarches a mission and gives it meaning by placing it into a perspective. In this sense it might be more correct to directly equate military missions with business objectives rather than visions. In the early 1990s Archie Norman and Allan Leighton of ASDA saw their first job as getting their vision right; this consisted of their mission, purpose and values. In his book *On Leadership*, Leighton is clear on where any leader must start:

> When I joined ASDA in 1992 it was a basket case. There were a thousand problems to sort out, but one of the first things that Archie Norman and I actually did was to spend days agonising over the wording of ASDA's mission, purpose and values...These underpin your activities when you start to build a company, and the biggest mistake a company can make is to change these core values.

The mission analysis process certainly translates into commercial life. For instance, with minor substitutions, military mission analysis readily becomes commercial vision analysis.

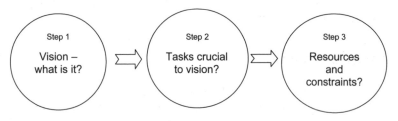

Figure 2.4 Vision analysis

TOOL 2: THREAT ASSESSMENT

In any military operation, correctly assessing the threat you face is a vital part of the planning process. I cannot see why assessing the competition in commerce is any different to that.

The threat we face is always determined by two factors; the capabilities of the opposition and that opposition's intended course of actions. It's a simple formula:

Threat = Capabilities × Intentions

In threat terms, 'capabilities' means the physical capacity to have an effect on us if utilized. Possessing a tank is a capability. If the tank doesn't fire it is a dormant capability, but if it opens fire it is dynamic and has an effect. Just having the tank is defined as possessing military power whereas the tank firing is the application of military force. Peacekeepers, as we were in Bosnia, try to use military power to get their way without having to resort to military force.

Competitors that have the capability to do you damage might or might not do so, depending on their intentions. However, competitors that have no capability to do you damage but want to attack you will not have the means to do so. Remember, though, that whilst capabilities normally take a long time to build, intentions can change overnight.

The skill comes in determining exactly where a prospective opposition sits in terms of its capabilities and intentions. As such, judgements can be out of date quickly and threat assessments must be constantly reviewed. I used the 'Threat = Capability × Intentions' formula just prior to my Bosnian deployment in 1992 and an unclassified version of the document I wrote is shown in Figure 2.5.

TOOL 3: ESTIMATE

The detailed planning tool used by the Army to assess a situation and plan what to do is called an estimate. Mission analyses and threat assessments may have already been completed so this next process, my third tool, helps to design a detailed plan. It consists of a number of steps.

1. Mission
   This is a repetition, as well as confirmation, of the mission. Hopefully, as a result of mission analysis what is required is crystal clear. Military missions are always written in an uncompromising and ungrammatical way. They use the imperative and are straightforward statements of intention, such as 'To Capture Hill X.' They are also as short and to the point as possible.
2. Factors
   Anything that might have an impact on the mission are factors. In military terms such factors normally include enemy forces, threat, strategy, involvement in higher plan, terrain, own resources, weather and timings. But such factors are never standard and vary depending on the situation. The key to whether they should be considered is to

UNCLASSIFIED

Copy ... of ... copies

Ops 1/CO's File

By: Lt Col Stewart
For: 2IC, Adjt, Ops, Int, List B
At: 0930hrs

On: 24 Oct 92

THREAT ASSESSMENT
BSA, HVO AND BiH FORCES

Force	Capabilities	Intentions	Threat
Bosnian Serb Army (BSA)	Successors of JNA. Warsaw Pact capability. Recce Pty attacked by MiG fighter. D-30 Arty range 17kms. T-62 and T-55 tks. No shortage of sups.	Most professional opposing force. Allowed recce pty with reservations. Not happy about UN presence. Opened fire on recce pty. Most likely to open fire.	BSA has respect for British. Few inhibitions about engaging UN forces or British UN forces.
Bosnian Croat Army (HVO)	Some JNA wpns. Tks (T-55) – few formed units. AA guns in ground role. D-30 guns.	Some ranks worn on uniforms. Cagey about UN presence. Recce pty involved in firefight but not deliberate. Likely to open fire if provoked.	Supported UN presence so far. Feeling is that HVO could open fire at us. Exposed being exposed to HVO without support.
Bosnian Muslim Army (BiH)	Few wpns; small arms and mors only seen. Few unarmoured vehs or tks (none seen on recce) Some AA guns but possess a lot of mines.	Most welcome force to UN. Very stretched and no formed units. Nothing seen of Mujahaddin units. BiH likely to support us.	Least likely to attack us but we should trust nobody. On recce threatened us on a couple of occasions.

R A STEWART
Lt Col
CO 1 CHESHIRE Gp

UNCLASSIFIED

Figure 2.5 Bosnian threat assessment

ask the question, 'So what?' If a factor has no impact on the mission then it is irrelevant and can be ignored; it is a distraction and has no importance to what you are trying to achieve. Each factor should point up some form of deduction. For example, on D Day in June 1944 high tides were necessary in order to ensure landing craft were not struck by obstacles on the beaches, and deductions suggested dates and times when the invasion of Europe could occur more easily.

3. Options

Here the possible options are highlighted. It is very tempting to decide on a course of action quite early in planning and then skew all thinking towards that course. But considering various options helps keep planning flexible. In Army written estimates, the advantages and disadvantages of each option are normally clearly spelt out. This third step ends when one or other of the options being discussed is selected.

4. Plan

Finally, the plan outlines what has been decided so that, if necessary, there is sufficient information to make a more detailed operational plan. In the Army the outline plan always repeats the mission and then suggests how a plan will be executed under headings such as a general outline (of what is to happen), tasks (for each team) and coordination (such as timings).

Below I have copied the template estimate format I always carried with me in my Filofax.

Although the exact form of a military estimate may vary depending on circumstances, the four key headings – Mission, Factors, Options

ESTIMATE
1.   **Mission**.
2.   **Factors**.
a.   En Forces.
b.   Opposition.
c.   Higher Plan.
d.   Ground.
e.   Own Resources.
f.   Weather.
g.   Timings.
h.   Communications.
3.   **Options**.
a.   Course 1.
      Advantages/Disadvantages
b.   Course 2.
      Advantages/Disadvantages
c.   Selection of the Best Course.
4.   **Plan**.
a.   Mission.
b.   General Outline.
c.   Tasks.
d.   Coordination.

Figure 2.6 Estimate format

and Plan – are normally there. I used the process time after time in
Bosnia. For example, I wrote such an estimate on 24 November 1992
when working out how I should get into Northern Bosnia from Central
Bosnia. In that case I used key estimate headings but felt I had enough
from it without detailing the plan. I repeat – decision-making tools are
there to help, not enslave leaders into a rigid format.

TOOL 4: NEGOTIATION

From the first moment I set foot in the Balkans it was clear to me that
I would have to spend a huge amount of time negotiating. Leading
negotiations is not easy and you need to be completely focused on
the issues in hand. My first practical exposure to negotiation came on
20 October 1992. Over a 24-hour period I negotiated the release of
two journalists as well as a Bosnian Croat soldier being held hostage,
and led six different negotiation sessions. By the end I was exhausted.
Serious negotiation is hugely tiring – in the military or in business. I
strongly believe that negotiation in business is a crucial skill, especially
for such activities as takeovers, mergers, strategic alliances, marketing,
partnerships and, of course, selling.

I will describe my first practical experience of battlefield arbitration
in detail in Chapter 12. Suffice to say here that after 20 October 1992
I wrote four headings in my Filofax which from then onwards I used
extensively in pre-planning. These headings became what I call Tool 4.
This template really helped me to focus my mind under pressure, time
and time again.

		Negotiation
1.	Aim.	What I was trying to achieve.
2.	Strength.	Of my and interested parties' bargaining positions.
3.	Weaknesses.	Of my and interested parties' bargaining positions.
4.	Approach.	How I was going to conduct the negotiation.

Figure 2.7 Negotiation tool

3

Preparation

THE BALKANS PART 1: AUGUST– SEPTEMBER 1992

Two days after my briefing by the MoD, I flew to Zagreb in Croatia with a reconnaissance party of ten people. I had little idea what my official mission should be except that we were supposed to help provide humanitarian aid in some way. But it was clear that how we operated would depend upon the ground situation. Brigadier David Jenkins, Director of Military Operations in the MoD, suggested we should try and get to Tuzla in Northern Bosnia. He had already been to Bosnia and thought the need for humanitarian assistance might be greatest there.

LANCASHIRE AND GLASGOW PART 1: NOVEMBER 1996

During my early business career, I was given the task of organizing a campaign to increase paper recycling in the United Kingdom from 5 to 10 per cent. I knew little about the subject and so I decided to spend two weeks on the road in Lancashire and Glasgow, visiting and working in paper mills and recycling companies.

The experience was invaluable preparation, as I learned how the whole process worked from the ground up. I think it helped too that I arrived dressed and ready to do shifts of work when those running plants obviously thought I was likely to be some sort of 'suit'. One manager said so to my face – adding that he couldn't see what someone like me was doing at his facility. I told him I was there to do just exactly what his workers did on a shift – hopefully learning from the experience. He laughed, and promised I would be aching by the end of the day. He was right. I was exhausted, but we parted friends and the experience helped me to understand the business better.

THE BALKANS PART 2: AUGUST– SEPTEMBER 1992

I hoped that my reconnaissance would give me sufficient information to decide how to prepare and train my battalion. At Zagreb we met UN peacekeepers for the first time. I was not impressed. Apart from a few British, French and Canadian officers most seemed to be along for a ride – especially the good pay and conditions. It was obvious that the so-called UN Protection Force (UNPROFOR) lived well. Comfort seemed a much higher priority than any idea of having an operational effect on conditions for the people of the Balkans. UN officers ate, drank and slept in the luxurious four-star Intercontinental Hotel. They drove brand new Land Cruisers to and from their very decent offices a couple of miles away, and most had never even ventured out of the city. I asked a senior staff officer what he thought we should do when we arrived in Bosnia, and he simply shrugged his shoulders. The omens were not good – especially as we were scheduled to come under the operational control of such people.

LANCASHIRE AND GLASGOW PART 2: NOVEMBER 1996

As I visited various paper mills and recycling plants I made a point of asking everyone I met how he or she thought recycling could be improved. One man suggested a very simple improvement. Instead of allowing incoming vehicles filled with waste paper to unload near the gate (which meant it had to be shifted again to where it was to be processed), incoming vehicles should simply take the material directly to where it would be fed into the recycling machines. It seemed a very basic change to me so I asked why he had not made the suggestion to his site manager. His answer said it all. 'He spends all his time in the office. He's never around and he hasn't asked.' I went to see the site manager and innocently asked why the waste paper wasn't going direct to his machines? I was told that wasn't my concern.

Exchanges like that give a clear indication as to why some businesses are more effective than others.

THE BALKANS PART 3: SEPTEMBER 1992

Our small reconnaissance party was determined to find a way that the British contingent could make an effective contribution, even if the UN had so far shown itself to be particularly inept. For a start we decided our aim on the reconnaissance should be to work out a way of deploying my battalion into a position in Bosnia or close to its borders. We wanted to find a place from where we might have real impact on the humanitarian situation.

Equipped with a few Land Cruisers lent to us by the UN we set off for Tuzla in Bosnia very early one morning. As we drove for five hours south-east from Zagreb we passed through several UN checkpoints manned by soldiers of various nationalities. Increasingly we heard artillery fire and the sounds of battle. Passing into Serbia we turned south and tried to get to Tuzla from the direction of Zvornik across the River Drina on the Bosnia–Serbia border. We planned to get into Bosnia from the west. But once over the River Drina our problems really began.

The Bosnian Serbs were happy to allow us to run around Serbia but as we tried to get near the front lines on Bosnian territory friendly relations faded rapidly. We were thwarted continually by aggressive and non-compliant Bosnian Serb soldiers who gave us the runaround. Stopped, threatened and searched frequently, we travelled up and down, round and back again – as close as possible to the front lines between Bosnian Serb and Bosnian Muslim fighters. We came under fire a couple of times and the whole situation seemed very dodgy. The viciousness of the internecine fighting and obvious targeting of civilians shocked us all greatly. In Bosnia anarchy was running rampant.

LANCASHIRE AND GLASGOW PART 3: NOVEMBER 1996

When I went into paper mills and recycling plants I was normally welcomed warmly. I always explained that I was there so that I could learn more about their business in order that I could help to get more paper and cardboard recycled throughout the UK. I explained I was not any form of inspector. The workers were normally pleasant towards me – even if they did sometimes regard me as something of an alien. Working with them for a while helped them to accept me. I told them that I was there to learn what the job was all about, so as not to make stupid recommendations in any report I wrote.

Twice I went on waste paper collection rounds. I saw the difficulties involved, and as we went round I talked to people about recycling. They wanted to recycle but collections had to be made simple, easy and regular as well as guaranteed. Such preparation resulted in a detailed report and eventual action plan.

THE BALKANS PART 4: SEPTEMBER 1992

A few days into the reconnaissance, whilst listening to the BBC World Service on our short wave radio, the early morning news announced that Serbia had been expelled from the UN. Deep in Serbia at the time, as a very small team with only side arms and wearing UN blue berets, we immediately felt uncomfortable and pretty vulnerable. This diplomatic expulsion, combined with the lack of cooperation we had encountered, convinced the MoD that we should try to get into Bosnia from another direction. We returned to Zagreb in Croatia.

The next day two RAF Hercules aircraft flew us to the Croatian coastal town of Split. We were directed to try and find a way into Bosnia from the south. For the next week we literally edged our way into the war zone. We had no real idea about where opposing forces were fighting or indeed the geography of the place. Blocked, held up, and sometimes shot at we were generally thwarted in anything we tried to do. But in the event we made the 240 kilometres into Central Bosnia to Vitez, and from there another 180 kilometres to Tuzla, which I thought to be pretty amazing progress considering the obstacles we had overcome.

We crossed some huge mountains, mostly on very poor tracks, on our journey to Vitez and Tuzla. I couldn't help worrying how I would get my battalion over such difficult terrain as winter was arriving. A Warrior armoured fighting vehicle on ice can rapidly become a 30-tonne sledge and there were some massive drops from some of those tracks.

But our reconnaissance and preparation did result in a relatively decent plan involving an approach into Bosnia from the south passing through Split on the Croatian coast. After two weeks travelling around, the reconnaissance party flew back home. A day later we learnt our deployment plan had been approved.

MISSION ANALYSIS

1. Mission
   - My first priority was to establish a workable mission, because the politicians had not been able to get international agreement as to exactly what we should do. I examined the two Security Council resolutions that established the UN in the Balkans. Basically they directed that any soldiers deployed were to assist in delivering humanitarian aid for the United Nations High Commission for Refugees and, together with the International Committee of the Red Cross, to help escort ex-prisoners to places of safety.
   - Taken literally we could simply have planned to put a Warrior armoured vehicle at the front and back of convoys containing aid or prisoners and tried to escort those columns to their destinations. Apparently some UN contingents interpreted their mission in exactly this way. But, as I saw it, that would not be effective. The various factions would simply not let convoys pass. To succeed I felt that our mission ought to be much more wide-ranging than simply being confined to convoy duties.
   - I believed that the main reason we were being sent to Bosnia was to save lives – anyone's life. Moreover, any action taken with that intention was not simply defendable, it was an imperative. Looking at what needed to be achieved, I felt that both the UN and British Government really wanted us to stop people being killed and to protect them. Unfortunately, owing to a lack of international political agreement, they couldn't say this plainly. I decided my battalion should aim to save lives. That was a simple, clear mission and one from which I could operate. 'To save lives' thus became my working mission. Eventually, after I had been

in Bosnia for three months, the MoD approved this mission formally – once politics had caught up with what was happening on the ground!

2. Tasks
   - I had to prepare my battalion for operations in Bosnia. This was a very practical problem. For example, on 21 August, the day I was warned that we were heading for Bosnia, only 5 per cent of my armoured vehicles were fully operational, because of a lack of spares. To sort out this problem we had to raid the supplies of every other British Army armoured infantry unit in Germany. The vehicles then had to be painted white and all their weapons test-fired and zeroed. This all took time. By the time we reached Bosnia, 95 per cent of my vehicles were fully operational – a very high ratio for armour.
   - I had to get my battalion into Central and Northern Bosnia before winter, and in effective shape to operate. It would take up to three weeks to transport our vehicles by ship from the port of Emden in Germany to Split in Croatia. Thereafter moving the armoured vehicles 220 kilometres into Central Bosnia would take a further two days – provided the weather was not too bad in the mountains.
   - We had to begin operations quickly. In fact, from the very first moment of arriving on the ground, even without armour, my officers and soldiers went to work getting to know what was happening and trying to influence events for the good. Often they did so at extreme risk to themselves.
   - We had to be recognized quickly by all sides as professional, effective and influential. Regardless of the poor record of the UN, we were determined to change that. In particular I was resolute that no roadblock should stop us. We would be threatened by nobody, and our response would be vigorous if attacked.

3. Resources and constraints
   Resources:
   - I was mandated by the highest authority in the world – the UN Security Council. This mattered greatly to me, and gave what I considered to be both huge moral authority as well as a tremendous responsibility to act properly. I made extensive and practical use of this licence, quoting it often.
   - Not only were my soldiers well-trained professionals, but they were also highly motivated. We were also armed and equipped with the Warrior armoured infantry fighting vehicle, with which we had great confidence.

Constraints:
- I would be a commander in isolation, unable to discuss things with, or seek guidance from, a superior because communications to the UN and indeed the British chain of command were not good.
- I would be operating a huge distance from both reinforcements and re-supply. In Bosnia my battalion would be on its own, as there were no other British units in the country. I had to plan to operate independently even if cut off by the weather and by fighting. In the event, at one time in the tour we were cut off for two weeks.

I made huge use of mission analysis to sort myself out. It gave me the means to work out where I should go and what I should do when I got there. Mission analysis got me ready for the war.

AN EGYPTIAN ODYSSEY: 1997

One day in 1997 I was asked if I would be prepared to fly to Egypt and assist the Cairo Opera House put on a performance of *Aida* in southern Egypt. The venue was to be the ancient Temple of Queen Hatshepsut, across the River Nile from Luxor. I leapt at the chance. But it was no easy option, as I quickly found out when I asked for direction as to what was expected of me. My role seemed exceedingly vague so to order my thoughts I turned to mission analysis using what information I had been given.

I flew to Cairo as soon as possible. At the airport I was met by a man holding up a board with 'Mr Bob' on it. He told me that I was going to meet 'generals' and I got into a rather battered Peugeot for a most perilous drive into Cairo. Eventually we passed through a sentry-manned barricade and arrived at a dilapidated block of offices. I was taken inside and ushered straight into a room where three senior officers in uniform were sitting on the far side of a large table. My place was clearly the empty chair opposite them. They were the 'generals' and very severe they looked.

They said nothing, so I introduced myself. I said I was 'Bob Stewart' and shook hands with each of them. They curtly introduced themselves in English and then looked me up and down saying nothing. In London I had been warned that my reception might be a bit 'prickly' so I was prepared for their reaction.

In my mission analysis I had decided that I might need different business cards. I had my usual card in English but in addition I had ordered three more – one a direct translation of my normal card in Arabic, the second a card in English using my military rank of colonel and lastly an Arabic version showing my military rank. I flashed out the Arabic military version, saying that it was a real honour for me to meet three generals who had spared time for a British colonel. There was a slight thaw.

I didn't know much about the Egyptian Army but thought I would try using what I did know. Had any of them been involved in the Suez Canal crossing operation during the 1973 Yom Kippur War, I asked? Two of them said they had. I then went on to say how much we, the British military, admired an operation that had employed high-pressure hoses to blast tank exits from the canal through the steep sand barriers on the Israeli side. Egyptian tanks had then pushed out into the Sinai Desert and made quite a large penetration. In truth it was a brilliant idea, which I had studied at the Army staff college. My approach worked, and suddenly they began smiling, and a rapport developed between us.

Things were much easier thereafter, and I managed to get answers to most of the questions highlighted in my preparatory mission analysis.

Later, I flew to Luxor, 300 miles south of Cairo, and established myself in King Farouk's old Winter Palace, now a hotel. For the next three weeks I worked alongside the performance's producer and with both police and army on the security plan. I even used my Army staff college handbook to work out how many coaches would be able to cross the River Nile by pontoon bridge in an hour! I checked and advised on facilities at Luxor Airport for the arrival of a Concorde flight direct from Paris.

President Mubarak's wife was to attend the first night, which required a very complicated security and movement plan. For my own security I was allocated a personal protection officer, whose professionalism was such that his pistol kept falling out of his waistband at the most inappropriate moments! I wrote out a threat assessment, based on potential terrorist capabilities and intentions, which I kept it in my Filofax.

A large part of the reason I was there was to advise on counter-terrorist attack measures, because the threat from terrorism was considerable. To be honest, I thought we were running quite a risk. Because of this I spent a lot of my time on the security plan. We totally rewrote that plan and kept it a closely guarded secret. We thought an attack during the President's wife's visit was entirely possible. After all, the terrorist group al-Gamaa al-Islamiyya, which had frequently mounted attacks, had vowed to topple her husband's government. Unsurprisingly, I was a little relieved when the few days of the performance went off without a hitch and I was able to fly back to London. Mission accomplished, I thought.

On 17 November 1997, 68 people, mainly Swiss and Japanese tourists, were killed whilst visiting the Temple of Hatshepsut. The Islamic extremist group, al-Gamaa al-Islamiyya, carried out the attack. I had been back in London a month or so. Police and Egyptian Army personnel engaged in a two-hour gun battle with the terrorists. During the firefight six gunmen and two policemen also died. I felt a little guilty because of my relief that it hadn't occurred on my watch!

PREPARATION – BEDROCK OF SUCCESS

Getting thoughts and requirements in order before launching into any activity makes obvious sense. That preparation involves gaining a detailed understanding of exactly what might be required. Mission analysis has always helped me do that. Also, where appropriate, mission analysis should be accompanied by completion of a decent reconnaissance. An old saying suggests that time spent in reconnaissance is seldom wasted. How right that is.

4

Intelligence

THE IMPORTANCE OF INTELLIGENCE

Huge efforts are made to obtain intelligence. Getting the intelligence right can be battle winning. In 1944 Adolf Hitler was adamant that the D Day landings would not occur in Normandy but would be in the Pas de Calais. Allied intelligence had used all its assets to make him think so, and Hitler swallowed it. He was utterly convinced that Allied landings would be opposite Dover. He was so convinced of this that, even after the actual invasion across Normandy's beaches, he maintained the main thrust would still come directly across the Channel. Many believe his decision not to commit his reserve panzer divisions to the Normandy battle but await the 'real' attack saved huge numbers of Allied lives. Who knows – if Hitler had committed his reserve tanks on D Day then maybe the Allies could have been defeated in Normandy.

Intelligence is normally an opinion, hopefully well informed – based on deductions from information or data. Obviously intelligence activities are a very important part of war fighting. Intelligence can involve spying, secret agents and even reconnaissance satellites, but for most units in the Army the best intelligence probably comes from their own patrols and analyses based on observation or contacts on the ground. That was certainly true for me in Bosnia. From the start I was promised satellite intelligence showing deployments of belligerent forces from the air, but such help never materialized. Luckily I managed to get what I required by other means.

In principle, the techniques for getting business intelligence are much the same as for the military; gathering public information about competitors or markets by visits, open sources or occasionally more discreet investigations. I suspect that many business executives would be surprised by the amount of information and intelligence on their activities that is freely available to those who wish to discover it!

THE INTELLIGENCE CYCLE

Facts are not intelligence, and they don't speak for themselves. They require both analysis and subsequent interpretation. The military call this process the intelligence cycle. It normally involves five phases: direction, collection, collation, analysis and dissemination.

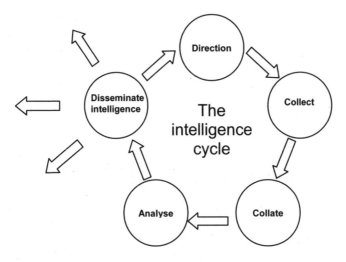

Figure 4.1 The intelligence cycle

The cycle starts with direction to various sources to collect information that might be valuable. That information is then collated and analysed to create intelligence, which is then disseminated or used to re-task sources to get yet further information.

GETTING INTELLIGENCE

I will demonstrate how intelligence is obtained using an example from my time in Northern Ireland. Soldiers there were directed to notice all sorts of information as they patrolled the streets. In their debriefing session afterwards they were always questioned by an intelligence collator. The collator's job was to record lots of information from the patrol, some of which might not seem important at all. One day a soldier mentioned that he had noticed the number of milk bottles outside a certain house had increased. An obvious deduction was that more people might be living there than before. That deduction, when investigated, resulted in the arrest of an on-the-run terrorist.

Industrial espionage is alive and well. As managing director of Security Express, my friend Eric Cooper-Key was asked to help solve a problem. A large company with head offices in London felt that a competitor seemed to know far too much about its operations. Eric and his head of security visited the firm. They noticed that an adjacent empty building had windows with a good direct view into the boardroom. When they went into one particular room in that adjacent building they found a high-powered telescopic camera on a stand. It was quite capable of photographing documents in the boardroom. On another occasion Eric found that competitors had wiretapped a client's boardroom.

BARRIERS TO PERCEPTION

Surprises happen, and we are often stunned when they occur. In retrospect, intelligence failures sometimes appear avoidable and we cannot believe we did not see them coming. Why is it that so frequently we simply don't spot the blinding glimpse of the glaringly obvious?

When I was at university I was fascinated by the work of Roberta Wohlstetter, an American academic. She specialized in examining intelligence mistakes. Wohlstetter noted that prior to any intelligence failure there was normally a huge amount of information available. She classified these as either 'signals' or 'noise'. A 'signal' she declared was a sign, a clue, a piece of evidence that points to something. 'Noise', on the other hand, was the background of irrelevant chatter that obscures 'signals'. 'Signals' may seem obvious after the event, but prior to it they are frequently obscure – lost in background 'noise'.

Wohlstetter analysed famous intelligence failures and suggested that even the clearest indications of an impending event were often missed because they were simply unnoticed in a mass of other information. Here is what she said about the failure by the United States to foresee the Japanese attack on Pearl Harbour on 7 December 1941:

> A close look at the historiography of Pearl Harbour suggests that in most accounts memories of the noise and background confusion has faded quickly, leaving the actual signals of the crisis standing out in bold relief, stark and preternaturally clear.
>
> (Rand Memorandum 4328, April 1965)

The information we receive is sometimes intricate, multi-faceted and hidden from all but the most penetrating and directed analysis. Indications to future events are always there, it's just that they have to be identified. We are overloaded with a mass of information. It often pours in at a tremendous rate and we have to be systematic in how we deal with it.

Additionally, no single person may have the full menu of all 'signals' required for accurate prediction. Sometimes all the 'signals' are there but they are not added together properly. Refugee reports about seeing missiles on Cuba had been arriving in the US Defence Intelligence Agency for at least 18 months prior to the Cuban Missile Crisis in 1962. But such reports were thought to be exaggerations. Then the crisis broke. It was a classic case of the 'cry wolf' phenomenon – warnings that are given so often that they cease to have meaning, until of course it happens!

There is also another very human problem that blocks accurate prediction. In reality all of us see only what we want to see. Everyone wears metaphorical glasses that distort or even block our view of what is happening to a greater or lesser extent. Nobody perceives things exactly the same way as anyone else. Absolute objectivity is simply not possible because it is always shaped by our preconceptions, and these differ from person to person. This particular revelation helped me a great deal when I was negotiating ceasefires in Bosnia. I kept reminding myself that, no matter how clear and simple the facts seemed to me, others, particularly those on opposing sides, would see things differently. Understanding this really did help me to keep my sanity in some fairly difficult negotiation sessions.

Some preconceptions can be devastating. At the beginning of 1973 Israeli intelligence believed that an attack from Egypt was impossible without Syrian involvement and Egypt's air force being able to seriously challenge the Israeli air force. Intelligence analysts felt neither of these assumptions was possible and so there could be no credible threat of attack. These two assumptions were so generally upheld by Israeli military intelligence that they even had a name: 'The Concept'. But Israeli intelligence got it seriously wrong, as the ensuing Yom Kippur War showed.

Likewise in 1950 there was ample evidence that North Korea was about to attack South Korea. But the 'signals' indicating this were simply not accepted because the CIA did not think it possible. In 1982 the Argentine invasion of the Falklands was foreseen by many sources – especially the US National Security Agency and British GCHQ in Cheltenham. But the UK's Joint Intelligence Committee dismissed such ideas as simply bellicose statements by the Argentine Junta.

Mental stagnation might also have a part to play. As the Berlin crisis developed in 1961 Western intelligence analysts thought the East Germans could block the whole of Berlin (as they did in 1948–49) but never just West Berlin. Like the Israelis in 1973, minds were fixed on only what they thought might happen. It seems to be true that, when conditions are uncertain, we often predict what we want to happen rather than what the evidence might suggest will happen.

We demand clear, unambiguous signals as guides to what a rival will be doing. But the reality is that if we want to get really good intelligence we must ask very specific questions that direct collators and analysts in a precise, exact direction.

A LONDONDERRY TALE

In 1978 I was an intelligence officer on duty in Londonderry, Northern Ireland. My job was to seek and obtain intelligence on terrorists operating in the city. One particular sniping team from the Provisional Irish Republican Army (PIRA) was being very effective in its targeting. Several soldiers had been killed whilst on patrol in the Bogside and Creggan areas of Londonderry. Obviously there was huge pressure for us to eliminate this very serious threat.

The problem was that we had very little intelligence on who might be involved. We knew that our soldiers were being shot at with the latest version of the M-16 rifles because we had recovered spent empty cases after shoots had taken place. Forensic analysis suggested that at least two different M-16s were being used.

As an intelligence officer I had over one hundred sources, more colloquially called 'touts' who, one way or another, gave us information on what they thought was happening in Londonderry. The vast majority of them were utterly unreliable and some were even dangerous as we didn't know who they really supported in the campaign. Despite our best efforts to milk information on the PIRA sniping team from them we had drawn a blank.

Every day I held a short meeting of my top team and each time we discussed how we might identify the sniper team. One day Colour Sergeant Ray Stretch suggested we plot on a map every shoot that we knew to have been carried out by this particular sniper team for the last three years. When we did this a pattern stood out. Most of the shootings had taken place close to the cathedral! I don't know why we hadn't done it before; we just had not.

We knew that prior to shootings PIRA teams tended to move the weapons being used into a short-term hide close to their intended firing point. It therefore seemed likely that cathedral property was in some way connected to the attacks, albeit without clerical consent. That seemed a good deduction, as the Army was never allowed to go into or on any piece of church property.

Further analysis turned up other interesting deductions. We looked at both the dates attacks took place as well as the times they occurred. There was another pattern. They seemed to occur every two to three weeks on a Friday or Saturday night between 10.30 pm and 2.30 am.

Now we had good intelligence. We could suggest that several M-16 weapons used in sniping attacks against us might be hidden on cathedral property – probably for a short time just before an attack. Additionally we could suggest both the days and times when attacks might occur.

I briefed the Commanding Officer on what we had deduced. Under the circumstances he didn't need much convincing that we should try and set up an operation based on this intelligence. He decided to stop all overt military activity during the greatest danger periods and instead to mount what we called 'lurk' patrols of only three soldiers in positions with observation of cathedral buildings. On the first night lurk patrols deployed, were not compromised and then returned. But on the second night we hit the jackpot!

As one patrol, led by Colour Sergeant Dave George, watched, a car stopped outside the cathedral's infant school, which, because it was church property, was out of bounds to the Army. Two men got out and went into the school playground. The patrol couldn't quite see what they were doing but they returned carrying what looked like a heavy sack. Colour Sergeant George challenged them.

The men piled back into their car and drove away fast. Our orders for opening fire precluded using firearms against them because the patrol's lives were not in danger. Nonetheless, they did not get away. We had anticipated this situation. Within a couple of minutes of passing a codeword over the battalion's radio net every exit from Londonderry was closed. Another patrol boxed in and arrested the men. Not only had we caught two PIRA gunmen red-handed but in the sack there were four of the most modern M-16 rifles ever captured in Northern Ireland. We were all terribly proud of our work that night as we had undoubtedly saved soldiers' lives by smashing a sniper team that had been most effective until then.

This story has several lessons. First it shows that even with little information, deductions leading to decent intelligence are possible. Second, it illustrates how team members can contribute innovative ideas. Finally, it reminds me of a quote attributed to Napoleon Bonaparte – 'Nothing is achieved without calculations. Everything that is not soundly planned in its details yields no results.'

GAINING BUSINESS INTELLIGENCE

Business intelligence is out there, too, and its 'signals' just need to be harvested, identified, collated, analysed and disseminated. The setting up of any form of business intelligence group is determined by its purpose. An obvious role would be to watch competitors and assess how effective they are currently and will be in future.

Intelligence information can come from customers, contacts, news-papers, journals and the media as well as more generally from the internet and competitors' company reports and magazines. But less open sources of intelligence, such as asset searches, due diligence, off-shore bank investigations and security surveys might provide some real intelligence nuggets.

The well-known SWOT (strength, weaknesses, opportunities and threats) analysis is a useful analytical tool. A SWOT matrix can help to bring the mass of information collected into some form of manage-able summary. It is likely that external trends, customer requirements and competitors' positions are known. From that a SWOT table can be

Strengths	Weaknesses
Opportunities	Threats

Figure 4.2 SWOT analysis

	Ourselves	Competitors	Customers
Strengths			
Weaknesses			
Opportunities			
Threats			

Figure 4.3 SWOT comparison analysis

calculated under its four headings (see Figure 4.2). It could be further refined to include the opposition and customer expectations (Figure 4.3).

A good SWOT analysis must be a living appraisal, revisited frequently to accommodate any changes in competitors' and customers' intentions. A threat assessment – threat = capabilities × intentions (Tool 2) is simply a variation on that theme. SWOT layouts can starkly indicate a real situation.

It may be that competitors are just too numerous to analyse easily. In that case perhaps the best approach may be to concentrate on the greatest threats. Company literature, websites and annual as well as analysts' reports are normally freely available to anyone. Most companies are keen to be highlighted in the media as it can be good, free publicity. When companies do this they usually try to emphasize why they are the best, and their unique selling points. Good for them, but it may be good for us too as such information really does give valuable intelligence.

Many companies put their intelligence activities within the sales and marketing division. Some, fewer perhaps, have a separate business intelligence function. Ideally, as a company grows, someone on the board of directors should take responsibility for intelligence. To be really effective and worthwhile intelligence should have its own champion. In the military the Chief of Defence Intelligence holds the highest rank possible – being a four-star general, admiral or air marshal – with immediate access to the Defence Secretary and Prime Minister. If direct representation on the board is not possible then whoever heads up intelligence should have rights of access to at least some board members, such as the chairman or chief executive.

Military intelligence cells have briefers, collators and analysts and I know some companies replicate this sort of intelligence organization. Intelligence team leaders need to know the business well and be respected throughout their company. Whoever it is should be inquisitive as well as hard-working. Being a good team player is pretty important and so, too, is being lucky!

It follows that the intelligence team must work well together and have a clear focus. Yet its remit should not be too constrained. The key to success seems to be to establish a practical, easy system that formally targets, collects, collates, analyses and disseminates the final product – intelligence – to those who need it. A business intelligence unit that fails to deliver on this basic requirement will not last long, but one that does deliver will be considered a hugely valuable asset that definitely contributes to the bottom line.

Ideally all executives should 'think' intelligence and report any piece of information they consider pertinent. When I was a managing director we didn't have the capacity to have our own dedicated intelligence staff. So I did the job myself and built up a personal intelligence database. I found it invaluable, particularly when briefing visitors from my parent company in the United States, or simply to recall what happened at the last meeting and what was discussed.

THE PLACE OF INTELLIGENCE

Military operational meetings place the latest intelligence assessments at the start of the meeting. Normally the intelligence is given verbally, as well as being provided in hard copy. That principle applies at all levels, from a battalion briefed by its intelligence officer to meetings of the defence council in Whitehall. Depending on circumstances these assessments can be short or highly detailed, but they are most certainly never omitted. As a managing director, I ensured that we started every internal meeting with some form of market assessment. I know some boards of directors have this as a standard operating procedure too. But I also know many do not. I wonder, if they did, whether they might be more effective?

5

Innovation

NEED – THE MOTHER OF INVENTION

I had to be inventive in Bosnia. General Sir Peter Inge, Chief of the General Staff, was just one amongst several senior officers who agreed. He also warned it was going to be unlike anything I had experienced before. Another general suggested that I would need to be 'flexible and resourceful in approach'. Then Martin Bell, the war correspondent, visited us to complete a report for the BBC. Kindly he agreed to brief my officers and warrant officers on what he thought was happening. His key message was that we should prepare to be surprised and shocked. He was so right.

Actually the whole British Army was unsighted on what might be required. We had no doctrine appropriate for peacekeepers in the Balkans as it was a novel, uncertain and very different environment. New thinking was certainly necessary and as the commanding officer that buck stopped with me.

A great deal of what we did in the Balkans was indeed created specifically for the place. Our deployment plan reversed the order of normal operational positioning. We put administrative troops into position in exposed locations before bringing in combat soldiers. We escorted convoys without being seen. We developed tactics to break through roadblocks. We thought out new operational procedures to cross front lines. Even the system of liaison officers we established was different. We totally reorganized the battalion to fit the job better. After so many years in Northern Ireland, where Army instructions were to avoid contact with the press, in Bosnia we encouraged it and allowed even the lowest ranking soldier to speak to any reporter. That worked beautifully – we received some amazingly good media coverage.

MAKING A DIFFERENCE

We had to make a difference in Bosnia. It was no good simply going there and being as ineffectual as some other UN contingents. I was aghast at their lack of impact when I saw them during my reconnaissance visits. We had to mean business from the start, strong both in intention and action. Bosnia was 'warlord' country. Respect there came from strength; weakness of purpose or deed would make us an irrelevance very fast. I too had to act as a warlord. Naturally I had to do so within international law, and the acting was simply that – I was no natural warlord.

It made great sense to try to create a climate of peace and stability in which to operate. If conditions could be improved, perhaps we would be able to escort UN convoys through areas with much greater ease. Indeed, if circumstances did get better, we might not even need to provide so much aid. To that end I felt we should also do all in our power to help stop the fighting and arrange ceasefires.

Some suggested that this interpretation was pushing our mandate from the Security Council to its very limits. Under it we escorted belligerent military units whose deployment in one area was upsetting the balance of forces, we transported commanders from one place to another in efforts to get the fighting to stop and we cleared mines, recovered dead bodies from front-line positions, evacuated casualties – both military and civilian – and crossed lines to help refugees move to safety. Some of these operations may seem a long way from the exact words of the Security Council resolution, which told us to run 'operations in support of the UN to deliver humanitarian aid'. But I disagree. Everything we did was ultimately in support of that aim and I felt we were not 'extending' the mandate but 'interpreting' it properly.

MORALITY IN INNOVATION

When I was considering any new idea I would always ask myself whether a course of action was essentially good or bad. If I felt it was morally defensible, then I would think about doing it. When Malcolm Rifkind, then Secretary of State for Defence, was visiting he asked if I had any problems with my rather weak mandate. I said it was not easy but I pushed it as much as possible. I explained how I looked at new problems. To start with it had to be legal. Then an action was either morally right or wrong, I explained. I remember saying that it normally crossed my mind to consider what people at home would want me to do. Malcolm Rifkind agreed with me and endorsed my approach.

CLEARING A ROADBLOCK

For some operations this 'right or wrong' approach needed some additional help. I had absolutely no mandate to force a passage through a checkpoint or roadblock, regardless of the consequences. Obviously I always hoped to achieve my aims by negotiation if possible. Launching a convoy towards a certain destination in the hope that it might get there eventually was not good enough – especially when intransigent checkpoints blocked the way.

My reconnaissance in the Balkans had given me plenty of experience of being blocked or stalled at roadblocks. Subsequently I spent many hours thinking just how we might overcome such problems. I needed to find a way to deal with intransigent commanders who refused us our right of passage.

As I thought about it I remembered a book I had read at university entitled *On Escalation*. It was written by an American academic called Herman Kahn and was about a decision-making method to deal with nuclear threats from the Soviet Union. Kahn had devised an 'escalation ladder' in which initiatives and responses ascended in severity from the bottom rung of a ladder to the top. I thought it might be adapted to my circumstances and played around with devising an escalation ladder specifically to deal with a difficult checkpoint or roadblock. A simplified version of what I worked out is shown opposite.

I was determined that we must not be stopped for long at any roadblock, and with that in mind issued a version of the roadblock escalation ladder to every vehicle commander. Then we trained ourselves to use it. We practised being patient, to negotiate using words and even military manoeuvres as well as a little bit of bluff in an effort to achieve our objectives.

For the most difficult roadblocks it was like a game of chess: each move calculated – at least on our side. Whoever was on the ground

14	Push through roadblock – firing if necessary
13	Push through roadblock – not returning fire
12	Use Warriors in military power manoeuvre
11	Senior officer visits and threatens
10	Use media on visit
9	Coercive visit to roadblock with Warriors
8	Officer visit to roadblock
7	UN officials visit roadblock
6	Escort local commander to roadblock
5	Request UN assistance
4	Meet local commander
3	Visit by local liaison officer
2	Visit with local police
1	Initial contact with roadblock commander

Figure 5.1 Roadblock escalation measures ladder

was supported with advice by radio. Getting through a roadblock was a team effort. Almost nothing was 'off limits' in an attempt to get our way. The 'game' would start when we were blocked. Next the checkpoint commander might be 'visited' and told that he was wrong to block our passage. It was made plain to him that we could not allow it. Perhaps we would then fetch the man's local commander to order the checkpoint to get it opened if, of course, that officer agreed to do so. Maybe we would arrive with CNN, Sky News or BBC camera teams. Twice, at very difficult checkpoints, having the press with me proved invaluable when I spoke to its commander. The conversation went something like this:

'Please will you open your roadblock? Your authorities have agreed that we can pass.'
'It's not possible.'
'Why not? All we want to do is to get aid through to people who urgently need it? Would you explain to the TV camera why not? Please would you speak slowly as one day this may be used as evidence in a court of law! Now can I ask you to talk to the reporter?'

That worked. Sometimes a camera can be far more effective than a gun! At other times we simply tried to overawe the soldiers at the road-block using the obvious military power of our Warriors.

On 18 January 1993 Bosnian Croat soldiers established a checkpoint with mines and vehicle obstacles between my base and Sarajevo. This was the only road that could get aid into the city and it was crucial to re-supplying the place.

Both fellow officers and I visited the roadblock and met the Bosnian Croat commander. He was adamant that he wouldn't open the check-point to UN aid vehicles because, he said, the Bosnian Serb front lines had advanced very close and his side needed to keep control of the road. Despite negotiations that extended for two days the commander refused to shift his position.

At 9 am on 20 January I visited the checkpoint again, telling the commander that now I had to open the route without further delay. Half-seriously, and trying to look the part of a warlord, I said, 'As I don't want to kill you perhaps you might reconsider?' He still wouldn't budge. I decided that we could wait no longer. We prepared a plan based on escalation ladder measure 12. A schematic of the diagram with which I briefed those taking part is shown below.

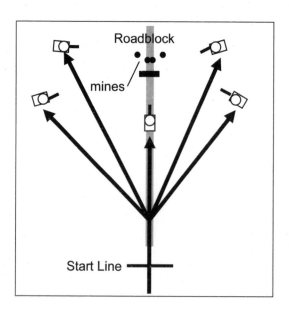

Figure 5.2 Plan to open roadblock

The plan had 3 phases.

■ Phase 1. Five Warriors, including mine, revved up their engines out of sight of the checkpoint. The noise could be heard miles away and most certainly at the roadblock. When I sent the word 'Go' over the radio two Warriors went left, two went right and then my own vehicle shot straight down the road – skidding to a stop just in front of the checkpoint. After a few seconds the word 'aim' was sent over the radio and all five Warriors rotated their turrets through 360 degrees before aiming their barrels at the Bosnian Croat checkpoint. It was a plain demonstration of military power.

■ Phase 2. This started when I gave the word 'up' over the radio. At that point I opened my hatch and got out of the vehicle. With a military interpreter I walked in to see the commander and shook his hand. Then I tried a bluff and congratulated him on 'winning'. I told him I had reported up the chain of command what an effective officer he had been. Taking out my hip flask I gave him some whisky and then asked for his help in 'saving my face'. I said I would leave a Warrior at the checkpoint to protect the place. 'As that was to happen there is no need for the mines to remain,' I said. I asked him to help remove them and went to do so. Bending down I asked him to help me. After a moment of hesitation he did so.

■ Phase 3. I moved a Warrior to the checkpoint as 'security'. Then the road was opened again.

A version of the escalation ladder is now taught as a roadblock busting technique for all peacekeeping operations. At least I have contributed a bit of innovation to British Army doctrine! Actually, the escalation ladder idea can be adapted to lots of other situations too – military as well as commercial.

BENDING RULES TO EFFECT

We used all kinds of new approaches to get our way in Bosnia – most of them untried until we had a go at doing them. Anything that might work was considered and we had lots of failures. I changed my organization frequently in order to be more effective and then altered it again as the need arose. Unusually for a commanding officer I would often work on my own or with one or two Warriors. That too was different. I did this so that I could go as close to the front lines as necessary or to get

Figure 5.3 Warriors on the move in Bosnia, 1993

to the nub of problems. But I was also perfectly prepared to delegate responsibility down to the lowest levels when necessary.

I told every soldier that he was a leader insofar as what he or she did had a huge influence on what happened around them. During pre-tour training I stressed the need for everyone to act on their own initiative when required. This particularly applied to opening fire.

As we prepared for Bosnia I was sent rules of engagement agreed by the Security Council. This was the UN bible as regards opening fire but was seventeen pages long. I read it carefully. It was utterly and completely impractical as a guide for soldiers operating in the field – particularly when they were in mortal danger. I wanted quick reaction and not a long mental revision of those seventeen pages. In Northern Ireland rules for opening fire were laid out on a short yellow card that had been very carefully drafted, checked by lawyers, shortened again and well practised over the years. But we had no time for that in Bosnia. I needed rules of engagement that were simple and well understood by everyone.

After a lot of redrafting I boiled down seventeen pages of directives and caveats into two sentences: 'A soldier can open fire if he/she or people under protection are in mortal danger. But, if there is time, soldiers should also think if, by doing so, the situation might worsen.'

Of course, any rounds fired must be aimed to kill. The idea that a soldier should shoot to wound is nonsensical. If the threat is great it is vital to neutralize an enemy completely and immediately. After all, if the threat was not great then why fire at all? And, although this may be distasteful to some, soldiers are taught to aim at the largest part of a human target, the chest. They do that because they stand the best chance of making a hit. It is far more difficult, not to mention dangerous, to try to hit the arm or leg of an armed opponent, because the chances of striking such extremities are much less. Once the decision to fire is taken any shots should be quick and lethal.

A PLATOON COMMANDER ACTS

When we were in a position to do something, we did. During the worst of the internecine fighting one platoon commander patrolled vigorously throughout his area with his four Warriors. To him it was clear that the Bosnian Croats were carrying out systematic murder. But every time he appeared their actions stopped – until he went away. When he went back he often found new groups of bodies in front of houses. He felt sickened, but could not be everywhere. He just did not have adequate resources for the job.

On one occasion he discovered every house in a road with bodies outside front doors – like garbage on dustbin collection days. Only once did he catch the perpetrators about to act. He noticed a group of soldiers advancing on a house that was burning. Then he saw that there were women and children in the house. Rapidly he swung his Warriors off the road. Positioning his vehicles directly in front of the advancing troops he ordered that all four Warriors point their main armament at them. To the advancing soldiers it looked like they could be exterminated. They turned and left, and the young officer took the women and children under his protection.

It was a very tricky action. That platoon commander's actions could well have brought us directly into the war if he had used his weapons. As I have previously stated, we were under unequivocal instructions not to get involved. But he felt he had to make a stand. He was determined not to yield and I think he would have opened fire if the soldiers had touched any of the women and children. In the event his firm response made the soldiers call off their attack. He probably saved the lives of nine women and children. That was a tremendous achievement of which he can be proud. It also demonstrated leadership and moral courage.

THE EYE OF THE STORM IS THE PLACE

We had one clear operational maxim: where there is a battle we go into the middle of it. Often our presence on the battlefield did calm the fighting. We would use any way we could to stop it. Once I put Lance Corporal Cleary, the battalion's bagpiper, on the roof. His playing was heard way down the valley and the fighting stopped as people listened to this extremely strange sound. The tune 'Highland Cathedral' had stopped a battle, even if only for a while. That simple act was innovative and it had an effect.

The MoD and UN Command stated that we could not get involved in the fighting, but nothing said we couldn't be there! If we were present, witnessing, in white vehicles (the colour of neutrality), and prepared to shoot if attacked, I felt our presence might just calm the situation. It often did so, too. In truth within the high protection of our closed-down Warrior armoured vehicles we were pretty invulnerable unless struck by an artillery or anti-tank round. We felt our way as we went, and the risk was normally worth it.

THE UNKNOWN SOLDIER

It often took a while for me to hear about individual actions. Towards the end of my tour Thomas Osorio and Payam Akhavan, both from the UN Centre for Human Rights, were talking with me about victims they had interviewed after being 'ethnically cleansed' from their homes. Thomas told me that they believed one of my soldiers had probably saved the lives of over one hundred people a few weeks before. I knew nothing about it until then.

Osorio and Akhavan explained that a large group of Bosnian Muslims had been forcibly expelled from their homes by about ten Bosnian Croat soldiers, who then set fire to their houses. The soldiers marshalled them into a large group of men, women and children before starting to push them into the woods. Everyone in the group believed they were going to be murdered.

Just at that moment a Warrior appeared close by. The people saw a soldier dismount from the turret. Alone and apparently unarmed the soldier walked through the woods and approached the group of soldiers. He appeared angry and was shouting at the Bosnian Croat soldiers in English. They shouted back telling him to mind his own business and get lost. Witnesses said the soldier didn't understand, or pretended not to comprehend what they said. He didn't move, all the time indicating that the group of civilians should be freed immediately.

The Bosnian Croats pointed their rifles at the soldier. It looked like he could have been shot. But the British soldier stood his ground, glaring, gesticulating and shouting. Then the soldiers started moving the group further into the woods but the soldier just shadowed them still shouting. The soldiers seemed unsure what they should do but stopped the group where they were. The British soldier just stayed around for half an hour or so, eventually getting into a gesticulating conversation with two Bosnian Croats.

After a while both the soldier and Bosnian Croats calmed down. The soldier tried to reassure the terrified civilians and indicated that he would stay with them. He did just that. An hour later the soldier was still there when the civilians were taken into a school being used as a detention centre. Representatives of the International Committee of the Red Cross were present and it was only at this point that the British soldier left.

What that unknown British soldier did was counter to his training. He was on his own, with no immediate back-up and well away from the rest of his crew in the Warrior. Yet he had taken the initiative, been extremely brave and had adopted a highly risky approach to saving lives. If someone had done that on an exercise prior to our deployment he would have been severely criticized for stupidity.

Thomas Osorio and Payam Akhavan believed that by his courageous initiative the British soldier probably saved the lives of over one hundred people. I had my suspicions as to who the soldier might be. When I asked my suspect directly he said he could not remember. He was a highly likeable, decent man. However, I reckoned it was him and made sure that later he was mentioned in despatches for other outstanding soldiering during our tour.

BUSINESS CREATIVITY

A major executive responsibility is to challenge conventional wisdom in a search for better ways to achieve ends. If leaders do not continually look for different ways to do business then they will get stale or lose their edge. Surely in this respect business is like warfare – the best side will win in the end.

Everyone in a company should be positively encouraged to make suggestions that improve any aspect of business, be it production, marketing, selling, human resources or whatever. I know many companies take positive steps, such as financial rewards, to promote the search for new ideas. But in truth there is no formula or tool that can really help innovation. That is simply not possible. Invention is very human. No machine has yet been able to innovate in the way a human mind can. In business, as in the military, the best chance of innovating is to employ good people who are quite prepared to try something different.

GREAT IDEAS

Innovative ideas can come from the strangest places. Some retailers I know snoop around small, quirky shops in the back streets looking for ideas. Other people travel widely, deliberately looking for inspiration. My own idea of an escalation ladder for use at roadblocks also came from a faraway place – my time at university.

Whenever or wherever that brilliant idea flashes into your mind, it should be immediately written down. How often have I heard a great joke? I tell myself that I must remember it, only to find that it has completely gone from my mind when I want to retell it.

One of my best ideas came when I was lying in bed late one night in October 1992. I was trying to think of a way to encapsulate exactly how we should behave in Bosnia and came up with the phrase 'controlled determined response'. We should always be controlled by international law in what we did, we would be determined in doing so and we would always respond in some way or other. I believe that phrase described exactly the way I wanted to operate in Bosnia and later I kept using it as a yardstick against which to measure operational planning there.

BRAINSTORMING OR FOCUS GROUPS

A public relations company I once worked for held many meetings during my time there. The vast majority of them were called brainstorming sessions or focus groups. After all the company's end product and main *raison d'être* was the production of ideas and plans to help clients do their business better. Here are a few observations I noted at such so-called creative events:

- Any meeting should start exactly on time and end as scheduled, or before if possible. It never seemed to happen like this though and used to irritate not just me but others who were just as busy as those who were late claimed to be. The best way to enforce decent timekeeping is to start bang on time and refuse to recap what has happened when latecomers turn up. They get the message fairly quickly.

- Keep meetings as short as possible. In Bosnia I ensured my daily conference never lasted longer than 30 minutes, and I do not see why normal focus-group meetings need go over that time limit. The first 20 minutes is the productive period anyway. Sometimes before I had a sneaking, perhaps unworthy feeling that some people used such meetings as a means of escaping real work!

- Some advocated convening stand-up focus-group meetings but I didn't like that much. For me it was an uncomfortable, obvious gimmick and not necessarily helpful to the generation of ideas.

- Whatever the meeting is about it should have pace, be interesting, even fun, and have a real point. If you leave a meeting and nothing has changed as a result then it was a pointless waste of time. Don't go next time if you can avoid it.

- Flip charts are useful tools, but are only that. I have always arranged meetings so that aids such as flip charts were readily available and often went through a great deal of 'flips' as we proposed, discussed, rejected, revisited and decided on what might or might not be a good idea. One technique is for each team member to take a turn on the flip chart, starting by drawing or writing an idea. But I have seen too many focus-group meetings where decorating the paper has too much priority. The purpose of the meeting is to get ideas that enhance business, not to compete with Picasso.

- Everyone should be encouraged and expected to contribute. If somebody said almost nothing in two consecutive meetings I simply didn't include them in the third.

- Bringing in fresh talent doesn't hurt. Sometimes a new eye and one unschooled in what has gone before can be helpful. Those that have been thinking long and hard about a project can easily become slaves to fixed ideas. It happens to everyone. Of course that is a major reason why business leaders so often call on outside consultants to help them. Once I remember I asked a cleaner who was working in the corridor to give a focus group her opinion on what we might do. My colleagues thought I had taken leave of my senses and they might have been right. It would have been great if it had worked.

Sadly it didn't, but it really sharpened up the so-called experts, who were bursting with suggestions thereafter!

■ One session may not be enough. For me several, short, sharp brainstorming meetings rather than one longer meeting are the best way to winkle out new ideas. Second and subsequent meetings should be equally brisk and to the point. People who are experts at crosswords say they often skip a clue they just cannot get and return and get it right later, when their brains have had a rest.

As ideas came and went I always kept a list of them. Sometimes an idea previously rejected became viable again if we tackled the problem in a different way. Nothing is wasted because it might work later. I repeat that 30 minutes is a good yardstick for length of meetings because people don't get too stale. Anyway, if the team starts to lose concentration its leader should see that and pack up.

A meeting about new ideas should be intellectually uninhibited insofar as everyone should feel absolutely free to express his or her thoughts, however crazy they may seem. As a rule of thumb I feel the ratio of good ideas to rubbish ones is about one in twenty or twenty-five. But it may require a lot of paddling in the mud in order to reach a nugget.

INNOVATION IN MILITARY HISTORY

David and Goliath

About a thousand years before Christ was born David, a shepherd boy, fought Goliath, the Philistine giant and professional champion, across a stream near what is now Amman in Jordan. As Goliath prepared for combat he chose his battle sword and expected to use it swiftly and with deadly purpose to dispose of his puny opponent. David, knowing Goliath would expect a sword fight, deliberately chose another weapon. He was an expert shot with the sling so he selected his pebble missiles with care and put them in his pouch. As Goliath took up his battle position and practised with his mighty sword, David carefully unpacked his pouch, put a pebble into his sling, swung the sling round and round his head and then let the missile fly. It struck with deadly accuracy, probably on Goliath's forehead, and he was killed instantly. David defeated Goliath by defying the conventional way to fight and using different technology. Not just that, he surprised Goliath.

The Battle of Crecy

I pass by the battlefield of Crecy in Northern France frequently as I travel to our house in Brittany. Every time I do so I am reminded of the fact that in 1346 about 14,000 English soldiers defeated possibly three times as many Frenchmen by changing the way the battle was fought. The French expected the battle to be primarily fought by knights on horseback, but that was not how King Edward III of England saw it. His army had the longbow, which, with its iron-tipped arrows, could pierce armour. Moreover, the English archers could loose off about 10 arrows a minute. As the French cavalry charged they were cut down by flights of arrows. The latest technology, longbows with their range, penetration and rate of fire, utterly destroyed the way the French envisaged what should have happened.

The tank

It was a British Army colonel who noticed that the only vehicles that could manoeuvre across the incredibly difficult terrain around First World War front lines were caterpillar tractors with moving tracks. Then he thought that if they were armoured they could also provide excellent protection for soldiers in the attack. His idea was taken up and developed by the government. The project was top secret, and even those working on it were not told its real purpose. As a cover story they were told the prototype equipments were water carriers. So the developers called them 'tanks' and the name stuck.

Tanks made their first appearance at the Battle of Cambrai in late 1916 but it wasn't until a year later that tanks were used to great effect in breaking through enemy lines. This British innovation became one of the greatest military inventions of the twentieth century. Tanks have been the main ground force element of most modern armies since. That original First World War idea had huge consequences.

The Battle of Britain

In 1940 Britain faced the greatest threat of invasion since the Norman Conquest almost 900 years before. German forces had occupied Belgium, Holland and France. Britain seemed at the mercy of Hitler's troops. As a preliminary for invasion Hitler determined that the RAF should be neutralized so that the Luftwaffe would have total air superiority.

Subsequently the Battle of Britain was the first major battle fought entirely in the air.

From June to October 1940 the RAF and the Luftwaffe clashed over England. The Luftwaffe began its assault on Britain with more than twice the 600 aircraft available to the RAF. Both sides were equipped with the latest aircraft technology. However, the RAF had a slight edge over the Luftwaffe with its new faster fighters, the Spitfire and Hurricane. The design and speed of both these aircraft meant that they could simply out-manoeuvre the opposing Germans. The RAF possessed another technological advantage. The new British invention of radar enabled fighter controllers to know when German aircraft were starting to cross the English Channel. The RAF were then concentrated into areas where the Luftwaffe were predicted to attack. Such leading-edge technology was a battle-winning factor which allowed the RAF to overcome the fact that they were vastly outnumbered.

INNOVATION IN BUSINESS

Changing culture

Altering the culture of an organization takes time. It doesn't happen overnight. In most companies its culture or ethos is deeply ingrained and will be difficult to budge. Company structures can change quickly but its culture takes far longer to amend. You can see and touch an organization but culture is like smoke – difficult to redirect easily. Of course it can be done; not easily, but it is achievable with consistent effort.

That effort starts by re-affirming or deciding on what really matters to the company's board of directors. This, of course, is where company vision reappears. Vision outlines a company's core values and governing business principles. Such values guide the mission of companies and become the yardstick against which all significant company activities are judged. Changing culture can have a dramatic impact on company performance.

In his book *On Leadership*, Allan Leighton wrote about his time as CEO of ASDA in the early 1990s. He believed that the change of culture within ASDA resulted in the ultimate value of the company increasing by at least 600 per cent within eight years.

Culture change requires the full participation of all employees. Companies like ASDA, John Lewis and Marks & Spencer make huge efforts to get every single employee to believe their part in the business is important. Such attitudes make employees feel valued. They work better, give their organization great loyalty and play a vital part in building and sustaining company culture.

Direct Line Insurance

Since it opened on 2 April 1985 Direct Line insurance has created a business with more than 10,000 employees, offering a range of personal finance products to more than 10 million customers across the UK and in Europe. Direct Line's innovation was to use the telephone as its main tool. At the time its approach was revolutionary because it cut out the middlemen and therefore its products were substantially cheaper. It also used readily understood language and was fast and simple. The company started with 63 employees and one call centre in Croydon, but now it has five call centres across the UK.

In its first three months of operation the company issued 9,000 car insurance quotations over the phone. Today Direct Line is the UK's largest direct car insurer and it provides over 13,000 quotes every day. One of its policies is sold every 10 seconds whilst a customer notifies the company of a claim every 30 seconds. Annually Direct Line receives over 22 million telephone calls.

Dyson International

Sir James Dyson's ideas have changed the way we clean our houses. He invented the dual cyclone bag-less vacuum, which works on the principle of cyclonic separation. It was a revolution – so much so that the word 'dyson' has now entered the English language for his particular form of vacuum cleaner. But he produced countless prototypes before he was able to take his product into the market commercially. Dyson developed his own formula to achieve innovation: 'Creativity + Iterative Development = Innovation.' Looking for a breakthrough involves a great deal of perseverance as James Dyson has said:

Never, ever give up. Make it very clear what you are doing and why you are doing it, publicly and internally. Sometimes you cannot make a big leap but only lots of little improvements. In the end it adds up to a big improvement.

Amazon.com

Amazon.com was able to use the early internet to pierce through the bookselling market and reach customers directly. It is now the largest online retailer in the United States with nearly three times the internet sales revenue of any other company. Founded by Jeff Bezos in 1994 it then launched online in 1995. After establishing its virtual bookstore it soon diversified to other product lines like VHS, DVD, music CDs, MP3 format, computer software, video games, electronics, clothing, furniture, food and toys. Currently Amazon has established websites in Canada, the UK, Germany, France, China and Japan. It even owns some ships. In 1999, *Time* magazine named Bezos 'Person of the Year', recognizing the company's success in popularizing online shopping.

Lastminute.com

Founded in 1998 by Martha Lane Fox and Brent Hoberman, the website lastminute.com was set up so that its products could be marketed almost universally on the recently established world wide web. It became an icon of the internet boom and then floated at the peak of the dot com bubble. Although it lost hugely with the share price slump in 2000, it has survived, going through various permutations, public and private, to this day. It continues to be different and distinctive in approach, as well as the first internet site visited by most people in the United Kingdom who want to make travel arrangements.

THE KEY TO INNOVATION

New technology is very much a catalyst to innovation. Those who want to be at the cutting edge must be more than ready to accept and employ it. Understanding just what new technology can do might indeed lead to an inspired business idea. Jeff Bezos, Martha Lane Fox and Brent Hoberman were all quick to realize its potential, and their rewards were enormous.

Clearly, leaders who want to promote new ideas and innovation must encourage their staff to think differently. Executives with open minds who consider alternative approaches and ideas are definitely those who are best for their jobs. Yet nobody can guarantee innovation. That inspired idea, the sudden thought, a flash of perception instigated by something seen, heard or read are rare. Neither are such new thoughts teachable.

Great innovation may be a recognition of the obvious, such as David's decision to fell Goliath with a simple pebble or Direct Line's use of the telephone. But it is not easy – not only does it require that new, ground-breaking idea and some luck but it is also requires something else. Ask people like James Dyson, Martha Lane Fox and Brent Hoberman what that might be and I bet they would all say 'Hard work!'

6

Planning

LEADING THE PLANNING

Leaders who think that someone else should design plans involving their organization are not up to their job. The person at the top has primary responsibility for developing plans and that includes being personally involved in their subsequent evolution too. After all, planning is where a leader's personal ideas, concepts and themes are converted into schemes for delivery.

My plan for Bosnia was designed so that we could take one step at a time. First we had to get all our troops, weapons and equipment to Split in Croatia. Then we had to get that lot over the mountains into Central Bosnia. Once deployed in Central Bosnia at Gornji Vakuf and Vitez we then had to get into the north – to Tuzla. The plan was simple in design although quite risky and difficult to execute. But it worked and that's the main point.

As a desk officer in the Military Operations Branch of the MoD in 1984–85 I spent a large amount of my time writing plans to deploy or recover Army units across the world. Normally this was a relatively simple, well-rehearsed procedure. We used a format that we followed almost exactly. This is obvious sense. Those who originate plans can be greatly helped by using a checklist, and those that receive such instructions can more easily follow what is to happen because they understand the system. Most businesses, too, would be far less efficient without standardized operating procedures.

MINIMIZE PAPER

As a military assistant to NATO's most senior serving officer from 1988–91, I found matters very different to my earlier MoD experience. There, within NATO's international political headquarters in Brussels, I often used to think that some officials and officers equated status in direct relationship to the length of planning papers they produced. Frequently such written verbosity was then translated into the home languages of all sixteen NATO members too. The entire NATO Headquarters could easily have been buried deep in the paper it produced. I suspect that matters are even worse now that NATO has expanded from sixteen to twenty-six members – all of whom probably demand planning papers in their own languages! Paperwork is meant to make life easier not more difficult.

I always liked watching ex-President Ronald Reagan perform when I saw him on television. Many people have suggested he wasn't very clever and was too undemanding in his approach but I am not sure I agree. I appreciated his straightforward and unpretentious, even folksy, manner. His simple way of explanation most definitely came from the way he had been briefed.

Apparently Reagan employed a planning technique that he called 'round-tabling'. He liked to thrash out different points of view on an issue with his advisers and relied only on a one-page briefing sheet. As President he insisted officials and staff condense a problem into one page, which contained four paragraphs entitled:

- Issues.
- Facts.
- Reasoning.
- Recommendations.

Reagan made as many as eight decisions an hour during staff meetings, affixing an 'OK, R.R.' next to one of the alternatives presented in recommendations. This made for very quick decision-making. Some people were highly critical of Reagan's one-page approach to decision-making but he was following a well-established technique. Winston Churchill frequently demanded planning briefings about wartime issues on one sheet of paper. Dwight D Eisenhower was another advocate of the short, precise decision brief. He used it both as Supreme Allied Commander and later as President of the United States.

Apparently the one-page approach is sometimes also used by Sir Philip Green, owner of BHS and Arcadia Group. It seems Green often ensures all he needs for many meetings is put on one side of A4 paper. If problems as complex as those faced by Churchill, Eisenhower and Reagan later, as well as Philip Green in business today, can be simplified in that way, why shouldn't others adopt systems that boil down problems to their essentials?

I fully support the 'short is beautiful' approach and particularly like the idea of a problem being dissected into Ronald Reagan's four constituent parts: issues, facts, reasoning and recommendations. Anything that simplifies is helpful. If you want to look at such quick decision-making in more detail I recommend *The One Minute Manager* by Kenneth Blanchard and Spencer Johnson.

THE PLANNING TEAM

In business a board of directors is obviously the ultimate company authority and must normally approve any significant decisions. But the real detail is usually left to a planning team.

The British government's 'board of directors', the Cabinet, has over 20 members and is chaired by the Prime Minister. This is simply far too large for sensible planning and the Cabinet has an extensive network of sub-committees in order to make the system workable. For example, contingency operational planning is delegated to COBRA. This sub-cabinet emergency operational group meets in and is named after Cabinet Office Briefing Room A in the cellars of Downing Street. The seniority of COBRA's members is intended to ensure it makes decisions quickly, and that what needs to be done is done. Of course, that is the essential *raison d'être* for all planning teams. COBRA meetings are frequently chaired by the Prime Minister or Home Secretary.

At battalion level my planning team normally included the second in command (my deputy), the operations officer (who organized the Operations Room) and the adjutant (who administratively organized the Battalion). Sometimes it also included the signals officer, the quartermaster and regimental sergeant major too. Essentially such a group was the usual compromise between being small enough so as not to get clogged with people but large enough to get the best advice.

In business I have rarely seen a planning team that does not involve the chief executive officer in one way or other. The remaining planning team members might include heads or representatives from divisions

such as sales and marketing, human resources, corporate communications and the legal department. Normally 'small is beautiful' is also
a good principle to follow in designing planning teams.

THE ESTIMATE PROCESS

In the Army I always used the estimate format (Tool 3) for detailed
planning. The outlines of such an approach have been covered in
Chapter 2. For Bosnia I wrote a full estimate on 25 October 1992.
Some of the information in this estimate was classified and much of

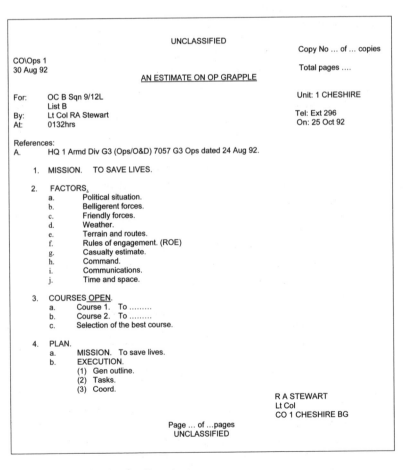

Figure 6.1 Estimate for Bosnia

the content irrelevant for this book's purpose. I reproduce the main headings by way of illustration. I apologise for those not familiar with Army terminology but I leave it in to give the copy authenticity.

My real estimate was very detailed and much longer than normal because of the complexity of what we were about to undertake. Let me make just a few points about what it contained to illustrate how estimates are used in the Army.

1. Mission.

   My mission was 'TO SAVE LIVES'. It was straightforward, simple and derived directly from my mission analysis.

2. Factors. (only deductions)

   Factors cover any issue that has a direct bearing on achieving the mission. But it is the deductions made from these factors that really matter. Deductions are the most important part of any estimate and are key pointers to the final plan. Rather than get into the detail of the factors I considered I will omit them entirely and only mention the key deductions.

   a. Political situation.
      - Politicians will get involved in what we will be doing.
      - The political situation is impossible to predict.
      - This will be an officers' war with them right in front.
      - We must find a way to successfully get through roadblocks.

   b. Belligerent forces.
      - We face a great threat. MoD suggests up to 25 per cent casualties.
      - The Bosnian Serbs are likely to attack us.
      - The Bosnian Croats might attack us if it suits them.
      - The Bosnian Muslims are mostly friendly but still not trustworthy.
      - Maximize the use of armour for protection.
      - Trust nobody in the Balkans until they prove their word.
      - We need liaison officers to become experts on a particular sector.
      - Get as many military and local interpreters as possible.

   c. Friendly forces.
      - Ten days after arriving we will be under UN command.
      - Only some fellow UN forces are effective or trustworthy.
      - We must plan to operate alone and without reinforcements.
      - Plan on company-sized bases in the North and South.

d. Weather.
  - Prepare for minus 20 degrees.
  - Cold weather clothing and equipment needed.
  - Armoured vehicles will need crampons on tracks.
e. Terrain and routes.
  - Route preparation will need two squadrons of engineers.
  - Recovery and re-supply assets in place on route over mountains.
  - Plan overnights on route into Bosnia.
f. Rules of engagement.
  - These need simplification.
  - Must be user friendly under fire.
g. Casualty estimate.
  - With 25 per cent possible casualty rate must have in-theatre hospital.
  - Casualty evacuation and care are top priority.
h. Command.
  - Under operational control of UN in Sarajevo.
  - But expect involvement of British chain of command.
i. Communications.
  - Our standard issue radios are unworkable in Bosnia.
  - We need different radio system – requested Euteltracs.
j. Time and space.
  - Plan on route from Split to Vitez taking two days.
  - Low-loaders should be used to take armour as far as possible.
  - Extreme driving care needed in snow and ice on mountains.
  - Commence move from Split not before 12 November.
3. Courses open. (no detail shown)
  a. Course 1. Three stage deployment with consolidation between each phase.
  b. Course 2. Still using phases but rapid move into Bosnia leap-frogging over first company and no consolidation.
  c. Selection of the Best Course. Course 2.
4. Plan. (outline only)
  a. Mission. TO SAVE LIVES.
  b. Execution.
  (i) General Outline. Three phases with a preliminary operation:
    - Preliminary Phase. B Squadron 9/12th Lancers are to clear and provide traffic control on route 10–11 November 1992.
    - Phase 1. B Company to move first to Gornji Vakuf on 12 November 1992. Battalion Headquarters to move with A Company.

  – Phase 2. A Company to move on 13 November 1992 and
    C Company on 13 November.
  – Phase 3. B Squadron 9/12th Lancers to join Battalion Head-
    quarters in Vitez on 15 November 1992.
c. Tasks. (individual tasks are not included here)

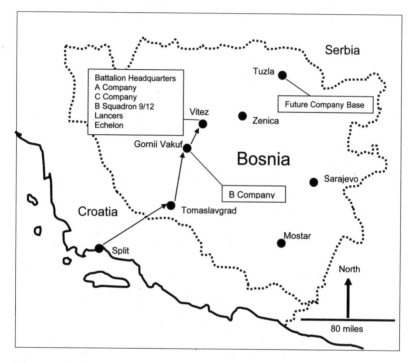

Figure 6.2 Operational deployment from Split to Vitez 10–15 November 1992

This plan worked, with slight modifications, and I managed to get my
battalion into its operational positions by 15 November 1992. During
the move over the mountains the ice had been extremely dangerous
but, although we had a few accidents, we lost nobody.

BUSINESS PLANNING

Unlike the Army there seems to be no universally suggested format for
business plans. Some companies have their own template but generally

most people determine their own way depending on what they are trying to achieve and for whom the plan is designed. For instance, a business plan to secure a bank loan might concentrate on how and when the company will repay the loan and a business plan to secure venture capital might assess initial investment, the effects of the loan and exit valuation.

In making a planning assessment a large number of factors will have to be considered.

The economy

What is happening in the economy both locally and nationally should be key factors in deciding business plans. Not only does the price of borrowed money matter greatly but so too do other factors, such as consumer demand. If you anticipate that interest rates are likely to fall then that may suggest that you could afford to create a more ambitious expansion plan. Seasonal factors might also have an impact. If you make products specifically to sell at Christmas, obviously you will need to take account of predictions on just how great customer demand for such products will be then, as well as what might happen thereafter.

Technology

We live in an era where the pace of technological change is incredible. In 1943 Thomas Watson, Chairman of IBM, stated, 'I think there is a world market for maybe five computers.' Now the earth probably hosts well over one billion of them! If you bought a new computer six months ago the chances are it's already obsolete – and a newer, faster replacement probably costs considerably less than its predecessor. It seems that it's all we can do just to keep up with technology, let alone understand its implications. This dramatic pace of technological change must have an enormous impact on all organizations.

Legal and political instructions and regulations

In Bosnia it was a mandate from the UN that ultimately determined operational strategy and tactics. My political and legal instructions were fundamentally wrapped in Security Council Resolution 770. In the same way all commercial companies have to work within strict legal and regulatory frameworks.

Executives must check carefully what rules and regulations apply to any prospective decision they might make. Sometimes, especially if working for a government organization, changes in executive political parties also have an impact. Employment laws matter. Assuming a company is big enough, in-house lawyers will be involved in almost all planning. If in-house lawyers are not available then outsourced legal advice may be needed. Most certainly, if redundancies are likely, a specialist employment lawyer will be required.

Time

Every plan must take account of time. It is a precious factor in planning. In military estimates time is frequently linked to space (a euphemism for terrain) under the heading, 'Time and Space'. The Confederate General Nathan Bedford Forrest in the American Civil War, and later General George Patton in the Second World War, summed up the need to calculate time against the yardstick of terrain by declaring that a winner 'Gets there firstest with the mostest'. Getting the timeline right is a crucial cornerstone of any plan.

In commercial planning, time considerations will affect factors like informing company employees about new initiatives, designing a new product, changing the means of production, producing new merchandise, delivering a product to the market and mergers and takeovers. No plan can ignore time factors.

THE BUSINESS PLAN

Once all factors have been considered then comes the whole point; preparation of the plan itself. Whatever format is used any business plan should include details of how the business is going to be developed, when this will occur, who is to do it, details about funding and expected financial returns.

Most business plans include the following:

- Executive summary. This is a précis of what you want to do and how you expect to do it. Getting this exact and correct is very important as it may be all a busy person reads.
- Outline business opportunity. This explains what your company is about, what you plan to sell or offer and to whom, as well as how you plan to do it.

- Marketing and Sales Strategy. This should include your unique selling points and why you think people will want what you have to offer. How you plan to market and sell your product should obviously be included too.
- Management team. Highlights the people who are most involved and explains why they are the best people for the job.
- Operations. This is the practical side of the plan. What, where and when you intend to do something is explained here. It might make sense to include facilities, production sites, human resources and IT information as well.

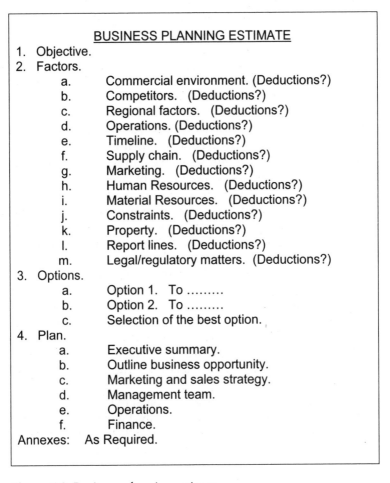

BUSINESS PLANNING ESTIMATE
1. Objective.
2. Factors.
    - a.   Commercial environment. (Deductions?)
    - b.   Competitors. (Deductions?)
    - c.   Regional factors. (Deductions?)
    - d.   Operations. (Deductions?)
    - e.   Timeline. (Deductions?)
    - f.   Supply chain. (Deductions?)
    - g.   Marketing. (Deductions?)
    - h.   Human Resources. (Deductions?)
    - i.   Material Resources. (Deductions?)
    - j.   Constraints. (Deductions?)
    - k.   Property. (Deductions?)
    - l.   Report lines. (Deductions?)
    - m.   Legal/regulatory matters. (Deductions?)
3. Options.
    - a.   Option 1. To ....
    - b.   Option 2. To ....
    - c.   Selection of the best option.
4. Plan.
    - a.   Executive summary.
    - b.   Outline business opportunity.
    - c.   Marketing and sales strategy.
    - d.   Management team.
    - e.   Operations.
    - f.   Finance.
Annexes: As Required.

Figure 6.3 Business planning estimate

- Finance. Here numbers really have impact. What is the cost, what is the expected gain and what special financial arrangements are needed?

TYPES OF BUSINESS PLAN

Business plan formats are obviously determined by their intended use and include:

- Quick sell or elevator pitch. A couple of minutes' summary that is meant to garner support or interest from its audience. Obviously it is short because the expectation is that the target audience will be available for very little time. The term itself comes from imagining you are in a lift with someone and only have the time the lift will take to reach its destination. Potential funders, customers and strategic partners who will only give you a short audience are likely targets for this quick sell.
- Presentation. A talk using slides, which aims to initiate interest and discussion by potential stakeholders. Often the oral presentation converts the plan's executive summary into interesting graphic form, which is probably accompanied by a printed script. If the plan involves new products these may also be demonstrated.
- Detailed plan. The main part of a business plan is a written, detailed account of what is being proposed. This is the main source of what is to happen and its primary target will be potential external stakeholders. Often the detailed plan includes an executive summary up-front that makes all the salient points very briefly.
- Operational plan. This is written for those who are to execute the plan. Normally this is an internal document that is crucial within the company but may be of little interest to anyone else. I have seen the internal operational plan included as an annex to the main business plan so that potential stakeholders can view it should they wish to be reassured that the plan is complete in terms of operational roll-out.
- Contingency plan. Sensible preparation should always include a look at what might happen unexpectedly. Preparing for a setback does not bring it closer but it will certainly help greatly when or if it occurs. More detail on contingency plans is given in Chapter 14.

7

Maintenance of morale

THE IMPORTANCE OF MORALE

High morale is unlikely without good leadership. Ensuring good spirits in an organization is a constant and enduring requirement for any leader. Good morale ensures that all members of a team have confidence and self-esteem, and possess the internal drive necessary to succeed. The leader's aim must be to make everyone individually and collectively at ease, with the spirit and self-discipline to do their jobs to the very best of their ability even when conditions are difficult or even harsh. In this respect I have always been terribly impressed by what I have read about General Sir William Slim's success in turning around the morale of British troops in the Far East from 1942 to 1945.

In March 1942 General Slim was appointed to command the Burma Corps, which had been chased out of Rangoon by the Japanese. Slim exploited his best talent – that of talking to soldiers and restoring their spirit. He possessed the 'common touch' of being able to level with his men, and get them to do his bidding. Although he still had to conduct a 900-mile retreat to India, Slim turned that from a disorderly panic into a controlled military withdrawal.

By May 1942 Slim's force had reached India and there, thankfully, the Japanese were halted. Slim insisted on jungle warfare training – even for headquarters staff. Prior to the Japanese invasion many of his troops had been little more than paramilitary forces in Burma. Proper jungle training provided them with a newfound confidence, while his pep talks added the motivation. His earlier service with the Gurkhas and troops of other nationalities paid off as he was able to speak to many contingents in their own languages. Later Slim reckoned that one-third of all his time was spent talking to his men, whose motivation he knew to be key to eventual victory. Morale leapt under General Slim's leadership.

In Bosnia I was very lucky. My soldiers were motivated most of all by the job they were doing. To the best of my knowledge, each and every one of them felt they were there to save lives. With regard to morale my job was simply to ensure it was as high as possible. For the first three months or so I was repeatedly told to compile a contingency plan for a rapid withdrawal from Bosnia. Actually, whether we stayed in Bosnia was very touch-and-go for quite a long time. I remember talking about a possible withdrawal to some soldiers and how I was under orders to prepare withdrawal plans. Their spirited and collective response was superb: there is no way we are leaving these people to their fates, they need us. I know that, if I had had to order a withdrawal, the soldiers would have done it. But it would have been a very difficult situation.

ASSESSING MORALE

Normally the morale of an organization is relatively easy to feel. It shows in the way people talk and act, and it can be sensed, often simply by walking around an establishment. This is the way senior Army officers normally assess the state of morale in units under their command. Commanding officers have sometimes been sacked outright because a visiting general thought morale and discipline to be poor.

The state of morale in a commercial organization is not exactly measurable but its presence is fairly tangible. In my time since the Army I have worked with many companies. The morale in those companies was normally pretty evident to me if I looked for the signs. One quick indication is to watch how leaders interact with their junior colleagues. There are a lot of clues in speech and body language – both ways. Respect is a two-way affair, and it's just as important to give as to receive it.

A person who has no interest in the job, who simply watches the clock, or who continually runs down colleagues or bosses is unlikely to have high morale and more than likely to be a rotten employee too. A little bit of whingeing may be par for the course but it should be just that – minor and meaningless. In the Army there is always a bit of moaning, almost regardless of circumstances. It's a characteristic of soldiers everywhere. They like having something to complain about, but normally it isn't very serious. The same probably holds true in most companies.

MORALE BEATS NUMBERS

Napoleon was one of the greatest generals ever. His thoughts on the importance of high morale were largely based on his own military success – at least until the Battle of Waterloo in 1815! He once wrote that 'morale is to the physical as three is to one'. Napoleon felt that high morale was always more important than inferiority in numbers. For most of my military career I remembered what Napoleon had said but had no practical experience of what he meant. Bosnia sorted that.

In the Balkans I was often questioned by various belligerent commanders as to how many soldiers I had under command. Of course I wouldn't tell them that but asked them in return how many they thought I had. Invariably they suggested I commanded between 3,000–4,000 personnel. In fact the number was about 750. It was only then that I really understood Napoleon's words. My 750 soldiers were perceived as being at least three times their actual strength. That was great. I was terribly proud that we had such an impact. It came about simply because my soldiers possessed both personal and collective confidence and high morale. Napoleon also called morale the 'sacred flame' that must always shine brightly. Obtaining and keeping that 'sacred flame' glowing involves hard work, dedication and professionalism by whoever is in charge.

ACHIEVING HIGH MORALE

Bustling, cheerful employees are normally a good indicator of high morale. You are lucky if you take on a position of responsibility and find yourself leading a successful, happy team that works like a well-oiled machine. The trick then is to sustain that, because morale can be variable. It requires constant hard work and its maintenance must never be assumed. Good morale comes about or is prolonged because everyone feels that they are valued and they know they are great at their jobs.

Yet many leaders could do so much more to improve the morale of employees. Occasionally I hear executives proclaiming that morale in their organization is poor. Sometimes they bemoan that nothing is being done about it. By such words they imply that fixing it is not their problem. They are wrong. Everyone should do their bit to improve morale – whatever their position in an organization. Running down an establishment or individuals in it can be stopped in its tracks if people simply don't do it. My experience is that killjoys are not popular for long if they never stop complaining. Most people just get fed up with those who are permanently negative.

CHARACTER

I believe British soldiers normally have a great, but often black, sense of humour. On the night of 6 December 1982, after the Ballykelly bomb in Northern Ireland, I told one of my soldiers, Lance Corporal William Bell, that we would have to cut off his legs where he was trapped. We just couldn't free him and the doctors were worried about the onset of gangrene. He answered me, 'One hell of a way to get out of the cross country tomorrow, eh Sir?' I was amazed by his courage and his ability to make a comment like that when he was in agony and lying on the dead bodies of his comrades. In the end we managed to free him without cutting off his legs, but a year later and after a great deal of pain and fortitude he had both of them amputated.

In 1942, when pushed back to India's borders, matters looked very bleak and total defeat looked extremely likely for General Slim. He summoned a meeting of his corps commanders to decide what they could do. When he met them their faces showed just how desperate were the circumstances. As the leader he felt he had to say something to raise morale. 'Cheer up,' said Slim, 'it could be worse.' One of the commanders just looked at him and said, 'How?' On the back foot Slim searched for something appropriate with which to reply. 'It could be raining,' he said. Half an hour later the monsoon broke!

General Slim's attention to the personal needs of his soldiers was legendary. He was particularly concerned about the sickness rate. In his memoirs Slim wrote:

In 1943, for every man evacuated with wounds, we had 128 evacuated sick. The annual malaria rate alone was 84 per cent per annum of the total strength of the Army and still higher among forward troops.

Slim took effective action to look after his troops. He sacked three commanding officers for failing to ensure their troops took their daily anti-malaria pills and instituted a strict anti-mosquito medical regime. By 1945 the malarial rate in the 14th Army was one in a thousand.

What, then, should leaders do to improve the morale of those he or she leads? In my opinion there are three main ways to do this:

- Demonstrate that people matter.
- Ensure that personnel are confident, professional and believe in their job.
- Instil pride and discipline, both collective and personal.

Demonstrating that people matter

Nobody likes being treated unfairly and they are quick to notice when matters are plainly wrong. Whoever is in charge should also perceive inequalities and get them put right as soon as possible. Correcting the big stuff may take time but little things can be sorted out quickly. In Bosnia my top team paid great attention to what we could fix fast.

- Letters from home, terribly important to soldiers, sometimes took three weeks to reach us. Post calls are always events filled with expectation. A letter matters, and conversely no mail is always a big disappointment. I demanded that the system be speeded up and quickly post started to arrive twice weekly.
- Food also affects morale. The master chef, Mr Straney, worked incredibly hard to ensure that it was not only plentiful and nutritious but also just what the soldiers liked. The cookhouse was normally open 24 hours a day to allow people returning from patrol to eat on demand and enjoy the process, thus relaxing. I attributed Mr Straney's contribution to morale as immense, and his award of the MBE for what he achieved was universally applauded by everyone.
- I placed a very high priority on finding a place where we could establish a bar, television and even some games tables so that soldiers could relax a little. The quartermaster identified a small hotel with a very large room, which we took over quickly. This became the junior ranks' mess. Next we found a place for the sergeants' mess and finally we identified somewhere for the officers. That priority order also mattered.

■ It took longer to establish proper lavatories, showers and a laundry service but these too were set up within three months. Anything that positively improves the standard of living has a definite impact on morale.

Taking an interest in and caring about subordinates is good leadership. But it can go wrong. During the First World War, Field Marshal Haig, a stern, unfriendly man by nature, normally inspected soldiers in complete silence. One day one of his staff officers tentatively suggested that it would be good if he were to talk to a few soldiers as he did so. On his next inspection Haig stopped and asked a soldier in the front rank: 'Where did you start this war?' The man replied, 'I didn't start this war, Sir. I think the Kaiser did.'

Remembering names is a basic requirement. When I was a brand new second lieutenant in 1970 I visited British Military Headquarters, West Berlin. Suddenly Major General the Earl Cathcart, the commanding general and cousin of the Queen Mother, appeared in the corridor. I tried to shrink away but couldn't do so before he reached me. As the 'great man' passed me, a lowly second lieutenant, he said, 'Hello Bob'. I had only met him once before and I was impressed. But what he did next had even greater impact. The general continued down the corridor and saw a German cleaning lady scrubbing the steps. He stopped, knelt down beside her and, using her name, asked in German how her sick husband was feeling. That was seriously impressive.

When I worked for various companies it was evident that top leaders who noticed and talked with their employees received much greater respect. Employees felt they mattered and were encouraged. As a managing director I made it a golden rule to allocate a sacrosanct 30 minutes every day to walking round and talking to the people who worked for me. Of course I knew their names, and I tried to remember the names of most of their families. Remembering who was sick at home or whose children were sitting examinations was second nature after Army training. It is basic care. So too are other simple measures, such as ensuring there are decent tea and coffee making facilities and a place where a break might be taken.

A leader who cares for those below will get it back in spades. Conversely, if the boss doesn't care for employees, why should they care about him or her? In business a 'happy ship' is very often highly competent, efficient and amongst the best in its business.

Confidence, professionalism and belief in the job

Collective confidence comes from a feeling within everyone that they can deal with any task well. That confidence is initially planted by good training. Infantry soldiers have to be good with their weapons and good at shooting. They must be fit, able to read a map and apply first aid as well as able to work in tactical groups on the ground. This is exactly what General Slim ensured by rigorous jungle training in Burma. Their confidence and professionalism grew in direct proportion to their increasing military competence. Slim convinced all his soldiers that they were more than a match for the Japanese and with that conviction came the realization that they were.

Obviously in business members of staff have to fully understand what they are expected to do and feel themselves absolutely capable of doing it alone. That's one form of empowerment. The best employees are those that feel that they, and they alone, are best at their particular job.

In the Army soft training is next to useless. Officers who believe that their men will be grateful to them for gentle instruction have little understanding of how professional soldiers, with genuine pride in their skills, function. Soldiers thrive best when under pressure and will have little regard for an officer who they perceive to be soft. They have to be stretched so that they push themselves to overcome difficulties. Achieving something that at first seemed unachievable hugely boosts confidence. That principle applies equally when training in commercial life. Away days and the like should not be soft options. Going home after a rigorous mental or physical challenge always gives rise to considerable satisfaction. Conversely, training that is far too easy suggests it's a bit of a waste of time and money for all concerned.

Training objectives should always be set. All exercises and instruction should then be assessed against such objectives and eliminated if they do not reflect them. I have often heard people comment that corporate training events were great networking opportunities as well as fun, but they should be more than that. Those that attend them should come away better at their jobs than when they arrived.

Instilling pride and discipline

Shortly after I returned from Bosnia I happened to see a television report of my battalion leaving our base in Central Bosnia for the last time. The cameraman was positioned so that he could record the Warriors departing. Then he focused on the driver of one Warrior just as it was passing him. Inside I could easily identify the driver. He was 19 years old and was saluting into the camera lens. It was a clear sign of pride. That soldier was very pleased by what he had achieved and his part in the collective endeavour we had all carried out over six months. He was proud to be in his platoon, his company and his battalion. His instinctive way of showing all this was to salute the camera. Saluting, to a soldier, demonstrates, particularly in this case, pride in doing a job well. It is exactly this feeling that all leaders hope to replicate throughout their organizations.

A lot of people hear the word 'discipline' and immediately associate the term with the military. They might also think of it as an alien, almost hostile word that has no connection to their lifestyles. There they are wrong. Each one of us uses self-discipline throughout our lives. Discipline is getting up at a set time for work. It is dressing in a certain way, even eating a proper breakfast prior to departure for work as well as getting to work on time and being prepared for the day.

Neither is discipline about shouting and bullying. That is an out-of-date image of Army life. Sadly there are always people who use their position to bully their subordinates, but that is as wrong in military as it is in civilian life. It merely reflects their own imperfect character and inadequacy.

I rarely gave a direct order to anyone. Either I discussed things with colleagues and we reached a consensus or I asked people to help me after I had made a decision. My approach was greatly influenced by the example of Brigadier Mike Dauncey DSO, who had once been recommended for the Victoria Cross. In 1944 at Arnhem, as a young lieutenant, Mike Dauncey was wounded several times and on each occasion when he reached the regimental aid post he thought others should have a higher priority. So he went back to the fighting. In his first wound he lost an eye, and his last injury occurred when a German stick grenade blew up and broke his jaw in two places.

Years later, as commanding officer of the Cheshires, he never raised his voice nor condemned anyone loudly or openly. He was truly a decent, quiet and strong man who had nothing to prove. His approach to discipline normally involved summoning a miscreant and in discussion with him suggesting that he, Mike Dauncey, had failed because such and such a thing had happened in his battalion. The soldier in front of him was normally so embarrassed by such courteous humility that he immediately owned up or accepted the blame for what had gone wrong.

Mike cared deeply about soldiers and his example engendered pride, determination and self-discipline in everyone he commanded. His was a different and somewhat unique way to lead, but truly effective.

Discipline suggests proper behaviour and correctness at all times. An indication that discipline might be poor in an army unit could be a bad record of drunken behaviour or a lot of absence without leave. Similar indications in a commercial company also might include high absenteeism, a large staff turnover or maybe high levels of bad-mouthing of colleagues.

A good company is one that is respected for the quality of its work and the standards it maintains. The same could be said of someone with self-discipline. In the commercial world self-discipline involves simple matters like returning calls and emails promptly, ensuring good timekeeping, producing reports on time, informing subordinates about what is happening and quite simply doing the job well. To me the words pride and discipline imply a cocktail of thoughts including confidence, professionalism, self-control, willpower, restraint and strength of mind. All these traits are fundamental to effective, dynamic operators in any walk of life.

THE FORCE MULTIPLIER

High morale is very much a force multiplier. I have already mentioned the effect that our morale and confidence had on the perceptions of local people and the belligerent commanders in Bosnia. But the same holds true in commercial life. An organization with high morale is normally an effective one and that directly impacts the bottom line.

8

Personal style

SOME HISTORY

When one of the greatest military commanders of all time, Alexander the Great, was dying in 323 BC they say that his soldiers were so desperate to see that he was still alive that he was floated past them, in great agony, on the River Euphrates. The physical presence of Alexander was of inestimable value to his army but, to the dismay of all his soldiers, he died soon afterwards. One of Britain's best military commanders, the Duke of Wellington, once put the numerical value of his greatest opponent, Napoleon, at plus 20,000 soldiers if he appeared on any battlefield. The simple appearance of Field Marshal Erwin Rommel amongst any German soldiers in the Second World War had an incredible impact on morale. What singled out Alexander, Napoleon and Rommel as incredibly effective commanders of men was not just their military wisdom and successes but also the style in which they led.

PERSONALITY MATTERS

Different people obviously have differing personalities. Character largely determines the way individuals act. In Bosnia I had seven majors reporting to me. All were of about the same age, background and training. But I knew that if I gave each of them exactly the same task they would all do it in a slightly different way. Actually how they might do the job was also one of my principal considerations when allocating tasks.

There is no blueprint character who will automatically make a brilliant leader. In the Second World War the command styles of generals Eisenhower, Patton and Montgomery were hugely dissimilar. Eisenhower worked by consensus, Patton often on impulse and Montgomery with arrogance and complete self-assurance. All three were highly successful commanders but none was the slightest bit like any of the others. Look at the latest American presidents. Bill Clinton is very different to George W Bush and Barack Obama is nothing like the other two. Each has his own unique character that governs how they perform.

Character is a product of genetics and upbringing. It is difficult to alter character, but style is a different matter. When I briefed Margaret Thatcher in Northern Ireland shortly after she took power she was very different in manner and style to the Prime Minister I listened to in the MoD some ten years later. Mrs Thatcher deliberately changed her manner by coaching. But it was more than that. Style is not a fixed asset. It can be changed or adapted to suit circumstances.

Like everyone else in command, I had my own style. Before Bosnia I thought that style to be congenial, open and somewhat democratic. I believed myself to be a sympathetic commanding officer and certainly not a hard one. But, as I prepared myself for the Balkans, I asked myself whether that sort of style would be effective enough for the challenge I was about to face? In truth I thought it would not.

I realized that I would probably need to make much faster decisions with less reliance on discussion before action. It was also obvious that I would be on my own without access to help and direction from above. The pace of war in the Balkans was simply too quick. In addition it seemed to me that I would have to be a much more robust, harder leader.

In consequence I spent a lot of time working out my style for Bosnia. The process I went through was not particularly comfortable. My failings seemed obvious to me; I knew me better than anyone else. I felt I was not robust enough and doubted my mental toughness to deal with the situation or a great number of casualties. In addition I was worried that my basic insecurity would show.

MY STYLE

I knew that sorting out my style of command in Bosnia was my problem alone. To that end I put myself under a private microscope. Nobody else was involved or knew what I was doing.

It is always difficult to accept personal criticism – even when it is well meant, constructive and kindly given. I started by looking at what my superior officers had written about me, because I had retained copies of my recent annual reports. The Army assesses officers against ten qualities and my 1991 report graded me as shown in Figure 8.1.

	Excellent	Very Good	Good	Weak	Supplementary Remarks (if any)
Zeal & Energy	x				
Reliability	x				
Commonsense & Judgement		x			
Intelligence	x				
Leadership & Man-management	x				
Tactical Ability	x				
Oral Expression		x			
Written Expression	x				
Organizing & Administrative Ability	x				
Tact & Co-operation	x				

Figure 8.1 Confidential report qualities 1991

In reality I knew that for someone like me most crosses should have been in much lower graded columns but, like everyone else, I was grateful when they were placed higher than that. However, I noticed that I received lower marks for common sense and judgement, and oral expression. Whether my senior reporting officer was right or wrong he had that impression of me and I took note of it.

Confidential Report 1991

> '*Lieutenant Colonel Stewart's first year in command has been far from straightforward or easy. His approach to command has been positive, very practical...* He has a caring style of leadership... He is also a touch verbose ...'

Confidential Report 1992

> '*This well motivated, thinking officer knows his battalion extremely well, resolutely looks after the interests of his soldiers – indeed if anything,* he has a slight tendency to wear his heart on his sleeve, *for which he is clearly much respected, even revered within the battalion.*'

Figure 8.2 Confidential report performance assessments 1991 and 1992

Every confidential report also contains a written description of performance. Extracts from my 1991 and 1992 reports, written by different senior reporting officers, read as in Figure 8.2.

After thinking again about what those reports said I accepted the highlighted criticisms. 'A caring style of leadership' (1991) and 'a slight tendency to wear his heart on his sleeve' (1992) are Army speak for 'A bit soft'. 'A touch verbose' lines up with the lower mark on oral expression in the 1991 report.

But I knew the best and most accurate judgement on me was by me. I could be really honest about this privately. So I returned to the Army's qualities template and wrote down what I really thought about myself. What I decided is shown in Figure 8.3.

I tried to be brutally honest. Not only did I need to be more confident, hard, practical and dominant but I also needed to prepare myself for casualties. Ten years before, on 6 December 1982, in Northern Ireland at Ballykelly, I had lost six soldiers from my company and I had been distraught. This time the MoD was warning me of a far higher casualty rate and I had to mentally prepare myself for that. In the end I wrote reminders of how to improve in my Filofax and carried it with me all the time.

I felt that in Bosnia I really had to lead from the front, and of course that would be more risky. It was likely that I could be a picked-out target for attack. Yet, in the highly uncertain conditions of Bosnia, I felt

Characteristics	My View of Myself
Zeal and energy	*Not fit enough. Over-enthusiastic*
Reliability	*Good*
Commonsense and judgement	*Self-doubt – need to control this*
Intelligence	*Be more practical*
Leadership and man-management	*Up-front more in Bosnia*
Initiative	*Be bold and think new thoughts*
Tactical ability	*Radical thinking needed*
Oral expression	*Verbose*
Written expression	*Good at this – use it to explain ideas*
Organizing and administrative ability	*Bored by routine*
Tact and cooperation	*More forceful to get own way*

Figure 8.3 My personal assessment

being in personal danger alongside soldiers would be crucial in keeping their trust and respect. In turn this would impact on their morale and motivation. In the event I was to discover that my leadership would require me to have a great deal more moral than physical courage. Let me give two such examples of this, which involved operations at Turbe and Srebrenica.

TURBE 1992

In mid December 1992 Captain Mathew Dundas-Whatley, the liaison officer for Travnik, told me that the Bosnian Serb Army was likely to expel a large number of Croat and Muslim civilians across the lines at a place called Turbe. He estimated that about 1,000 refugees might be involved. Turbe was a small village eight miles west of my headquarters and on the front lines. I was told that when this last happened a few people had been shot to encourage the others to flee across no-man's land.

Turbe was a very dangerous location. On 1 November 1992, shortly after we had first arrived in Bosnia, a BBC cameraman had been shot and killed at Karaula, east of Turbe. It was really the most hazardous place close to us, where all three belligerent forces fought continuously. We had put considerable effort into getting to know the area. By mid-December 1992, even I had crossed the lines there twice before – to talk with Bosnian Serb officers on the far side.

Figure 8.4 Mine clearing, Turbe

I spoke to the United Nations High Commission for Refugees (UNHCR) representative about a possible operation to escort civilians across the lines. He told me that he was hidebound by a direction that they could not get involved with activities that could be construed as helping with 'ethnic cleansing'. Moreover he said that 'technically' we also would be aiding this if we helped people to move across the lines. But, I argued, if we don't do it people could be killed like last time. No matter, he responded, he could not get directly involved in assistance to any side which wished to push people across front lines. The Head Delegate of the International Committee of the Red Cross (ICRC) had a similar view as well, despite my repeated arguments that we needed to ensure the safety of civilians.

I decided to ask for advice from the British chain of command and sent a signal explaining what was happening, the attitude of the international agencies and an assessment of the risks involved. The response I received can be paraphrased: 'We believe that you as commander on the spot should be allowed to decide what to do but on your own head be it.' In short, you are on your own buddy!

It made me think. On the one hand I had freedom to do the operation if I wanted but, if it went wrong in any way, I knew my head was on the

---

	1 CHESHIRE Bn Gp
See Distribution	Vitez
CO/Ops/Pers	212030 Dec 92

MISSION ANALYSIS
REFUGEE PROBLEM – TURBE AREA

1. Mission. To save lives of displaced persons about to be forced over lines at Turbe.
2. Tasks.
   a. Impose ceasefire in advance so that all can cross lines in safety. Make use of BiH resources and commercial radio stations to impose ceasefire.
   b. Position troops at front lines. Maybe do not cross lines in armour.
   c. Negotiate and take charge of civilians from BSA for crossing.
   d. Return with displaced persons. Many vehicles might be needed.
3. Resources and Constraints.
   a. Resources.
      (1) B Coy available with 4 Pl on standby. Soft skinned vehicles from Garage.
      (2) Area LO (Dundas-Whatley) good contacts with BiH and known to BSA.
      (3) Use Bosnian Serb interpreter.
      (4) UNHCR and ICRC agree to be involved but 1,000 metres behind front lines.
   b. Constraints.
      (1) Keep to ROE.
      (2) No agreement as yet with BSA.
      (3) Risk analysis required.
4. Outline plan.
   a. Mission. To save lives of displaced persons crossing over lines at Turbe.
   b. Execution.
      (1) General outline.
          Orders: 212300hrs
          Phase 1: 4 Pl into posn.
          Phase 2: CO plus B Coy HQ into posn.
          Phase 3: Cross lines and recovery op.
      (2) Timings.
          220900   Phase 1 begins.
          221100   Phase 2 begins.

R A STEWART
Lt Col

Figure 8.5 Mission analysis for Turbe operation

block. Yet I felt I could not just sit there and watch a potential tragedy happen. I decided to authorize, plan and lead the operation myself.

My mission analysis, written on 21 December 1992, is shown in Figure 8.5.

I used every trick I could to make sure that we would be as safe as possible and that a ceasefire would be imposed. To start with I went on the local commercial radio station (which I knew was received both sides of the line) and said we were going across the lines and why. Then I used a radio to break into the Bosnian Serb Army radio net and stated much the same. They were not amused! Finally I warned Lance Corporal Cleary, the piper, that he would be required to play at the front lines when we crossed. It was amazing how far the sound of bagpipes could carry in the mountains of Central Bosnia. When they are playing few people can ignore them!

At 11 pm on 21 December 1992 I issued orders for the operation. These were fairly straightforward and, as was my normal practice, I used a diagram, which was photocopied and distributed to every commander.

The next day four Warriors began their move into positions on the front lines at 9 am. Two hours later the rest of us moved up. Once there I checked that the front lines were quiet and then took two vehicles across no-man's land, clearing a couple of minefields as we did so. That day we recovered over 1,000 refugees. When this reported up the British chain of command I received a congratulatory signal from the MoD. I wondered though, given my superiors' hands-off approach, what sort of signal it would have been if things had gone wrong?

Figure 8.6 Negotiating with the Bosnian Serbs with interpreter Dobrila Kolaba (killed July 1993)

SREBRENICA 1993

By mid-March 1993 the Bosnian Serb Army had completed the encircle-
ment of the Bosnian Muslim town of Srebrenica in Eastern Bosnia.
Throughout this operation the Serbs had been merciless in shelling
the place. Many civilians had been killed. Over the airwaves by radio
we could hear pleas to the outside world for assistance. The UN
commander, General Philippe Morillon, was determined to do something to help.

Soldiers from my base in Tuzla had already opened a route through
the front lines towards Belgrade. But to reach Srebrenica meant we
would go well outside our operational area. From that front-line crossing point it took about four hours to reach the town of Srebrenica by a
very circuitous route. But General Morillon, escorted by a detachment
of B Squadron 9th/12th Lancers, managed to get to the town. They
came under intense fire on arrival.

With no power to stop the attacks on Srebrenica by the Bosnian
Serb Army General Morillon decided that we should evacuate as many
children, women and old men as possible. But trying to negotiate a

Figure 8.7 Mission analysis while flying en route to Tuzla in March
1993

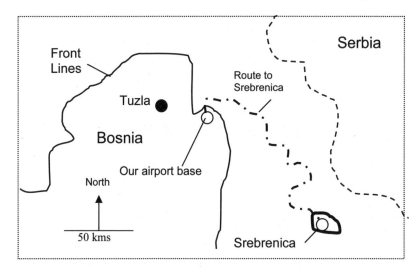

Figure 8.8 Srebrenica in March 1993

way cross-country using trucks at first seemed impossible and highly dangerous, because all road transport was likely to be attacked.

The only way that seemed quick and relatively easy, although still very dangerous, was to use helicopters. Through the national chain of command back to MoD I requested the use of British helicopters to fly across the lines and pull civilians out of Srebrenica. My request was almost instantly turned down. For good measure I was told not to overstep the mark and to stick to my operational area in future. But we had to do something.

A way forward came when I was speaking to a French liaison officer. He suggested French Puma helicopters might be able to do the job. Within hours I had French air support and the first helicopters were moving into and out of the besieged town. Refugees started to be air-lifted from Srebrenica and the full story of the horrors they had endured started to come out too. What we heard increased my determination to do all we could to help these poor, wretched people.

A BBC reporter asked me directly what was happening. I knew I was on very dodgy ground here. I explained that I had asked for British helicopters to help with the air evacuation from Srebrenica but had been rejected because it was considered far too risky. Then I mentioned that we did have some helicopters – from the French! Within hours a BBC report was broadcast in London and shortly thereafter British Sea

King helicopters were flying into Srebrenica – direct from an aircraft carrier in the Adriatic. Although nobody ever took me to task for what I had done I knew I had crossed a line. On the phone a senior officer said I was a bit too maverick; the kiss of death to a career – especially in a peacetime army!

STYLE REALLY MATTERS

If style does not matter then human beings are redundant. In a machine-run world training and performance could be a simple matter of procedures being followed to the letter. Army officers and business executives could be robots programmed to follow set procedures regardless of circumstances without human intervention. Follow that logic and there would be no need for leaders anyway, as everything would be pre-planned. Of course that is absurd and it will never happen (I hope). Leadership most certainly requires style. Thankfully none of us are exactly alike in character or the way we lead. Does style really matter for a leader? You bet it does!

9

Tasking

STYLISH TASKING

In June 1940 Winston Churchill tasked the Special Operations Executive to 'set Europe ablaze' with resistance to Nazi Germany. Many exceptional men and women, including my mother, went through exhaustive training to do just that. Churchill's exciting words gave out a task that was both a huge challenge and incredibly dangerous for those that took part. Setting the task, whether stirring or mundane, is a clear function of leading.

Of course, leaders must ensure that everyone in their teams is briefed and understands precisely what they are required to achieve. Poor tasking leads to poor results so getting it right from the start is very important. 'Don't argue, just do it' is a popular civilian view of military tasking. I won't say it doesn't happen sometimes but it is very rare because, except in the direst emergency where indecision could be fatal, such a method can be very counter-productive. I have given straight, no-argument orders in my time but I always much prefer to ask rather than order subordinates to carry out a plan.

In my view, tasking should also be very personal. Note the emotive language Churchill used when establishing the top-secret spy organization being formed to 'set Europe ablaze'. The best leaders are very keen to communicate the style and manner in which missions should be carried out and not just the mechanics of what they want achieved. Inspiring is best done in person. Standing in front of their teams, leaders have the perfect opportunity to explain exactly the way they envisage a plan unfurling, how complications might be dealt with and the manner in which they should be carried out.

On 13 August 1942 General Montgomery arrived at the desert headquarters of the 8th Army as its latest commander. The 8th Army was not in good shape and morale was low as it had been forced back almost to Egypt by General Rommel's German forces. Shortly after he arrived Montgomery briefed his new staff officers. He did so without notes. From the start he went straight for the throat:

I do not like the general atmosphere I find here. It is an atmosphere of doubt, of looking back to select the next place to which to withdraw, of loss of confidence in our ability to defeat Rommel, of desperate defence measures by reserves in preparing positions in Cairo and the Delta. All that must cease. Let us have a new atmosphere.

Montgomery then went on to detail exactly what was to happen and how he saw the future. Apparently the mood became electric within seconds. Those listening were quickly convinced that their new leader had the answers and they would turn defeat into victory – which they did in battle two months later.

For my part I remember one commanding officer giving an incredibly good and exciting briefing prior to an operational tour in Northern Ireland. It was definitely a special event during which he explained not just the mechanics of what we were to do but also the style, atmosphere and even the panache with which he expected us to do our business. It was showmanship, but most certainly memorable and effective. I left the briefing crystal clear on what was required as well as the way I was to perform my duties.

In Bosnia I considered briefing and communication to all members of my battalion to be even more vital than for conventional operations. I put great emphasis on each soldier being able to make his or her own decisions when it was necessary. Repeatedly I told everyone that they were all leaders because whatever they did mattered and would have consequences. Obviously if soldiers are so empowered, they must know exactly what is planned and their part in it.

CONSISTENCY

I have already explained that Army instructions from one level of command to the next follow an established and well-defined pattern. It is designed to be consistently familiar to everyone receiving instructions. When instructions are given out it makes sense for any leader to do so in a readily recognizable form. There is often a lot of tension when really important news or tasks are delivered so it helps recipients greatly if they don't have to spend time dealing with unfamiliar formats.

The mission detailed in a superior's tasking is not necessarily the same for everyone. Very often each person's individual mission is determined by the exact task they are allocated. For example, a director of sales and marketing is briefing her team. She states that the mission or objective is to raise sales by 20 per cent in the next year. The marketing executive is then told that his task is to increase advertising by 100 per cent. That objective, to double advertising, is his particular mission in support of the overall mission of raising sales by 20 per cent. In any tasking meeting the most important information that all present need to know is exactly what will be their part in the plan.

INITIAL TASKING

Tasking needs to be unambiguous, understandable, workable and timely. This last aspect is particularly important when urgency is required. As soon as possible after being detailed for an operation, commanders in the Army are taught to pass on a warning of what is going to happen to subordinates so that they can start to prepare for it. This system of warning orders is a standard operational procedure. I always used a set format divided into three parts:

1. SITUATION: What has happened?
2. ACTIONS: What are we to do?
3. SUPPORT: What help is anticipated?

The warning order I sent within 30 minutes of reaching my battalion headquarters on 21 August 1992 is shown in Figure 9.1. Note that this warning order contained few detailed directions – it couldn't, because I didn't have them then. But its purpose was to alert people to what was happening and give out as much information as I knew at the time. Within the warning order I stressed the need to start specific activities,

```
FROM:    CO
TO:      LIST B
         FAMS OFFR
         BRIG INF                              211837 AUG
92

WARNING ORDER

ONE. SITUATION. AT 211030 AUG 1 CHESHIRE PLACED ON
STANDBY FOR PEACEKEEPING OPS IN BALKANS. EXACT
BALKAN DEPLOYMENT UNKNOWN. CO TO MOD BRIEFING 22
AUG.

TWO. ACTIONS. ALL LEAVE CANCELLED. PERS CONFINED
TO FALLINGBOSTEL AREA. TRG TO CONC ON SHOOTING,
VEH PREP AND MEDICAL.

THREE. SUPPORT. 2IC TO COORD ALL PREP AND TRG. BRIG
INF TO ASSIST IN PREPARATION FOR DEPLOYMENT. PRE-
DEPLOYMENT TRG EX AT SENNELAGER LIKELY.

         Bob Stewart
         R A STEWART
         LT COL
         CO
```

Figure 9.1 Warning order for the Balkans

such as range work, vehicle preparation and first aid, immediately. Although I knew little about the operation, such concurrent activity is normal service practice, so as not to squander available time.

FORMAL ORDERS

In the Army formal orders are given out for operations as soon as possible. Sometimes they take time to prepare because they are more detailed and require considerable coordination with outside units or agencies. However, the format used is standard from a section of eight soldiers to an army corps of many thousands. In actual fact that format, shown in Figure 9.2, is now also standard throughout all twenty-six NATO nations.

Immediately prior to receiving verbal orders participants are familiarized with the area in which the operation will take place. Traditional Army descriptions of areas or ground are quite formulaic. They go from left to right, starting with the near ground then middle distance and then terrain on the horizon. Obviously more attention is paid to

MILITARY ORDERS FORMAT

DESCRIPTION OF TERRAIN

1. SITUATION.

    a. Enemy forces.   (Include intelligence information)
    b. Friendly forces.   (The overall plan above us)
    c. Attached & detached.   (Who joins and leaves us)

2. MISSION.   To .... (Always short and to the point)

3. EXECUTION.

    a. General outline.   (Brief description of the operation)
    b. Tasks.   (For each individual – can be a mission)
    c. Coordinating instructions.   (Which apply to everyone)

4. SERVICE SUPPORT. (Mainly logistic matters)

    a. Transport.
    b. Rations.
    c. Ammunition.

5. COMMAND AND SIGNALS.

    a. Command. (Who is in charge and when)
    b. Frequencies. (For radios)
    c. Code words.
    d. Nicknames.

Figure 9.2 Military orders format

any part that is considered important or vital during the forthcoming action.

The formal orders process begins with an analysis of the current situation. This starts with 'intelligence' on the enemy forces or opposition likely to be encountered. Known strengths, dispositions and intentions are dealt with in as much detail as considered necessary. Thereafter 'friendly forces' includes a description of what our own side is doing and in particular what other units are to achieve, especially their objectives. Finally this section concludes with details of which other units are to join the forces involved and indeed which units are not involved in the operation. The scene set, formal orders start to explain the plan in detail.

This starts with the key to everything; the 'mission'. Military convention directs that missions are always given in the transitive, which is a short phrase of what must be done. Ungrammatical, as short as possible and without the use of conjunctions, which might confuse, the mission statement is, by convention, repeated twice verbally. My mission for Bosnia was just three words: 'To save lives.'

After that comes the detail of how the operation should be carried out. This is the so-called 'execution' part of the orders process. It starts with a 'general outline' of what is to happen. Then the 'tasks' section is where each component part of the team is told exactly what is to be its individual mission in the operation. The final part of this section always contains 'coordinating instructions' where information common to everyone is included. Timings are an example of what might be given out under this section.

'Service support' means exactly what it says. This part of orders is where the administrative requirements are outlined and it is where details of matters like transport, rations, ammunition and any other logistic requirements are given.

The last part of formal orders is dubbed 'command and signals'. Again this is self-explanatory. Here details of who is in command, for what, when and how are given. The signals part covers matters such as radio frequencies, headquarters locations and their moves. Other control mechanisms, such as code words and nicknames, are explained here too.

DISSEMINATING ORDERS

In the Army tasking is cascaded down rather in the manner of pyramid selling. As a battalion commander I would brief my company commanders and headquarters staff officers. They in their turn would brief their officers and non-commissioned officers and so on right down to a corporal briefing the eight soldiers in his section. It has been a tried and tested method over the centuries and it works.

Such tasking is best done verbally and in person, or remotely by radio or even in written orders as the situation on the ground demands. The advantage of tasking face-to-face is obvious. It is far more personal and normally allows opportunity for questions with explanations as well as comment from those who have to do the business. If a warning order has been possible, participants in an operation are likely to have a pretty good idea of what will be expected of them, so what is being tasked will not be entirely new.

In an armoured infantry battalion, such as the one I commanded in Bosnia, orders given over the radio are normally listened to by everyone

Figure 9.3 Briefing the advance party at Vitez in October 1992

concerned. So a subordinate commander may only need to add his own ideas to the overall action plan for his team. Naturally radio orders are much shorter than more formal ones. For these there is an even greater requirement for precision and clarity.

I have always taken a certain amount of pride in the way I briefed people – normally making it a point not to use a note but to have the confidence to say what was to happen, unaided by props. Of course, most of what I said verbally would be included on notes that I passed out. But being able to detail what is to happen without using a piece of paper clearly shows that whoever is doing the briefing knows what he or she is talking about.

But sometimes paper instructions are absolutely vital. Once, late in the evening of 22 December 1983, I was given 18 hours notice of a visit to my company base in Northern Ireland by Margaret Thatcher, then Prime Minister. In my warning order by secure telephone call from Headquarters Northern Ireland the Brigadier told me that under no circumstances was I to tell anyone else until two hours before the Prime Minister's scheduled arrival at 2.10 pm the following day. That order gave me a huge problem.

I could hide some preparations. For example, electronic sweeps of surrounding streets or cleaning up the base were activities we did routinely. But there was precious little time to put fully briefed protective patrols into effective positions. I knew I had a real problem with time. Then I had an idea. I would draw what I wanted to happen on one sheet of paper and then photocopy it so that everyone could be given a copy of it as soon as 12.10 pm arrived. I closed my office door and spent two hours or so working out what to do. As part of that process I imagined myself 500 feet high in the air and then drew my plan on a piece of A4 paper. I photocopied my work, and gave it to every single person involved exactly two hours before Mrs Thatcher arrived. In the event the visit went off like clockwork.

In Bosnia I was insistent that I had a daily meeting with subordinate commanders who were close enough to attend easily. I was ruthless about time – with very rare exceptions the daily meeting would take no longer than 30 minutes. If officers could not be there because of distance or the pressure of operations it was a clear indication to me that I should go and visit them myself.

The easiest and indeed the best way to explain a task is to show those involved the ground over which action will take place. Failing that, film or photographs can be used for familiarization. Simple little tricks help, too, such as placing participants in the relative positions from which they will execute the plan. Then there is the possibility of using models. Obviously, the more realistic the model the more useful it will be, and they have their place in business too, where a model of a new product or prototype can help people visualize the task in hand.

COMMERCIAL TASKING FORMAT

I have always used Army methodology in my own business activities and with that in mind I have drawn up an outline tasking format that might suit most if not all business activities. The headings are my own but they can easily be dropped, swapped or altered to suit a particular situation.

```
COMMERCIAL TASKING

1.  SITUATION.
    a.  The competitive environment.
    b.  Company strategy/directions.

2.  TASK.  To .......

3.  PLAN.
    a.  Outline.
    b.  Individual tasks.
    c.  Coordination.
        (1)  Timelines.
        (2)  Joint actions.
        (3)  Meetings.

4.  ADMINISTRATION.
    a.  Finance.
    b.  Product supply.

5.  RESPONSIBILITIES.
    a.  Director responsible.
    b.  Report lines.
```

Figure 9.4 Commercial tasking format

10

Supervision

PLANS CHANGE

No plan survives contact with the enemy.

Helmuth von Moltke, chief of staff of the Prussian Army for 30 years in the late nineteenth century, was obviously referring to military strategy. But it could easily apply to business too. Plans do not take care of themselves. They need to be massaged and altered to respond to changing circumstances. They also require constant supervision and need to be flexible. History has shown time and time again that rigid plans are liable to fail.

Great play is made in military academies about the requirement to create surprise on operations, and this is a firm principle of war for everyone – not just ourselves. So why should we not expect opponents to put just as much emphasis as we do on achieving it? In military or business operations it is both prudent and good practice to expect the unexpected.

That is why plans should never be set in stone or inflexible. I don't think I have ever been in any military action that has gone off as originally designed. Actually the Army expects problems on all its operations and thus normally includes contingency plans for when they do arise. The principle of thinking through what could go wrong and making contingency plans makes sense in any profession.

On 6 June 1944, D Day, many German Panzer divisions, particularly 21st Panzer Division centred near Caen, were unable to move because Hitler had not given the necessary authorization. His staff refused to wake him to tell him about the invasion in Normandy and nobody had delegated authority to take decisions when Hitler was unavailable. This contrasted directly with the approach taken by Montgomery, who also normally insisted on eight hours of unbroken sleep a night. But he delegated executive responsibility to his staff officers so that he could continue his unbroken rest in the knowledge that they would do his bidding. He had told them what he expected and how they should react to the unexpected in some detail.

ARMIES MARCH ON THEIR STOMACHS

Napoleon famously announced that an army marches on its stomach. He meant that a well-administered army stood the best chance of success because its soldiers were able to concentrate on the fight. He was right.

We put a great deal of effort into organizing how we were set up, replenished and administered in Bosnia. Little details mattered. For example we knew that normal, healthy, active young soldiers needed at least 3,500 calories in a 24-hour period and this was the basic planning building block on how much food we needed daily. In the same way we anticipated the possibility that we would be cut off from replenishment for a period of several weeks and therefore had to have enough combat supplies, which included petrol, diesel, oil, ammunition as well as food, to survive such a famine. In the event this happened. For two weeks our main supply route was disrupted. But it had no effect on the pace of our operations because we had anticipated it.

REORGANIZING THE TEAM

A properly organized force is one that is designed to take knocks and be reorganized quickly in response to events. Over 700 officers and soldiers is a large number of people to supervise directly, and of course I didn't do that alone. British infantry battalions are all organized to the same basic pattern, although that does not mean they cannot adapt to new circumstances.

I changed my organization constantly in Bosnia in order to maximize operational effectiveness – moving personalities as well as sections and platoons around in response to events. Reacting to what has happened by reorganization is very much a part of a leader's supervisory responsibilities.

The Army designs its operational structures so that its leaders at all levels have a maximum of about ten people to control. This makes sense and very much reflects traditional military logic. A corporal commands a section of between eight to ten soldiers in the same way that a decanus in the Roman Army commanded ten legionaries.

I had a total of six company-sized groups commanded by majors who ran their teams using between four and eight officers. In their turn these officers used non-commissioned officers to organize their soldiers. This system had functioned well enough for our role in Germany. A commanding officer controlling about six majors running companies of one hundred plus officers and soldiers was traditional and had served the Army well since time immemorial. Company commanders would run their companies using platoon commanders in charge of about 36 soldiers. Each platoon had three sections of about 8–10 men. That basic hierarchical structure made sense, worked and remained the core of my battalion organization. However, I thought that Bosnia called for some changes in the way that structure operated.

■ I designed a system of liaison officers who would be allocated to specific areas of Bosnia to become our experts in that particular sector. Captains, mainly company second in commands, were extricated from their current jobs, and reassigned to this crucial role. They deployed with the advance party. Their responsibility was to get out on the ground, identify who were the local military and civilian personalities and then get to know them. When the main body of my battalion arrived, these liaison officers should know the ground and local situation well enough to give invaluable advice to company commanders assigned to their sectors.

■ I decided that in rotation one platoon or troop would also work directly for me. This was of course a reserve force, which made absolute sense, but it was also my own personal team who would be available for tasks at a moment's notice, such as escorting VIPs or armoured protection for liaison officers who normally had only two Land Rovers.

■ I created specific small teams responsible for: interpretation (we hired 15 local personnel), civil–military (CIMIC) relations (dealing with local groups), and public relations (at one stage I had 102 correspondents directly accredited to me by the MoD). The teams

Figure 10.1 Prime Minister John Major talks to Captain Richard Waltier, the Adjutant, on 22 December 1992

were to have an effect far greater than their small sizes would suggest. Interpreters were crucial assets and we really needed them to accompany every large patrol. The CIMIC Team performed very well by helping local people, especially during battles. Our public relations team even had its own Saturday night television show at prime time on the local station.

■ With a formal warning from the MoD that my casualty rate could be as high as 25 per cent I was in a very good position to ask for extra medical officers and facilities. In particular I requested that a field surgical team should accompany us, as casualty evacuation from Central Bosnia was likely to be impossible. The MoD agreed and in consequence two surgeons, an anaesthetist and three general practitioners with supporting staffs were deployed with us. To start with we established an eighteen-bed ward and operating theatre in the assembly hall of the school that became our headquarters at Vitez. The most a battalion could normally expect would be one general practitioner as the regimental medical officer (RMO). Actually we were also allocated another two RMOs as well.

CLARITY ON COMMAND

In fact these changes turned out to be a substantial change to the way infantry battalions normally operate. Individuals and teams were soon accustomed to being moved around as necessary, but I tried very hard not to dislocate the underlying basic organization of the battalion. For good practical reasons everyone was administered by their original company, even if they were working with someone else.

Whatever the operation, I made absolutely certain that the person in command of it was clearly designated and had full ownership of the assets given to achieve objectives. I decided on the best person to carry out the task and announced who was to command. Occasionally this resulted in a more junior officer operating with someone more senior under their command. I thought this might cause me problems but, in practice, it didn't because normally everyone saw the sense of such an arrangement. Again this was not normal Army practice – except perhaps with the SAS or other special forces.

EVALUATING THE SITUATION

Not only was the battalion controlled via the majors below me, but I also got direct reports from the liaison officers – although I was careful to ensure that they were not my spies and that once attached to one of my subordinate commanders they worked for and to them, not me.

My direct reports, the six majors, were the primary means by which I tasked, controlled, coordinated and evaluated what was happening when I did not have direct experience of events. But there were several other ways too. Four officers had particular responsibilities to be my eyes and ears – my second in command, then the adjutant, operations and intelligence officers. Most important of all, the regimental sergeant major, Charlie Stephens, as the battalion's most senior soldier, was a direct link to the sergeant's mess and all junior ranks. Finally I was with the soldiers a lot and I encouraged them to tell me how they saw it. They normally held little back when they did so!

The most effective means of knowing what was happening at any moment was the radio net, which was multi-stationed and operated instantly. This was the basic means of gaining information and issuing instructions direct to those in action. Unfortunately our radio nets were hugely erratic and inconsistent. In Germany the normal battalion radio net used very high frequencies (VHF) but in Bosnia the mountainous terrain more often than not blocked the 'line of sight' requirements of that range of frequencies. Communication via high frequencies (HF), our back-up, was hardly more reliable because that required atmospheric conditions to be appropriate for bouncing radio signals back to earth from the ionosphere in exactly the right place. That was it. We had no other means of communicating to and between troops deployed on the ground. Before I went to Bosnia the MoD had promised me at least a few 'euteltracs-type' radios, which used satellites, but we never received them. I have always felt let down on this matter.

But I also had other means of checking what was happening. Without doubt the best of these sources were journalists. I have already mentioned that at one time there were 102 of them officially attached to me. I grew to like and trust them more and more as the tour progressed. Sometimes journalists would brief both me and the intelligence section about what they had witnessed. I also had good relations with United Nations High Commission for Refugees (UNHCR) and International Committee of the Red Cross (ICRC) officials. They too were a means of gaining information. Indeed when we first arrived in Central Bosnia, in early November 1992, an ICRC delegate spent several hours in my intelligence section marking front lines and belligerent positions onto our maps. The delegate had been given special authority to do so because we were United Nations troops operating in a neutral capacity. This information was invaluable for briefing our early operational patrols.

Other great sources of information were the various belligerent sides that seemed more than happy not only to point out the positions of their opponents but also their own as well. This seemed very odd to me. But I suppose it shows that they trusted us, or perhaps they were simply naive in their understanding about what should be military secrets. It was, of course, great from my point of view but I made absolutely certain that access to exact front-line positions was appropriately classified in my base.

There is nothing better than personally gained knowledge of what is happening. In both military and commercial life visits are probably the best way of getting up to speed on the reality of what is happening. Some top executives deliberately spend as much as two days a week with customers or front-line managers. Alan Leighton of ASDA argued that if he knew what customers thought and what is happening in his stores then he should have a pretty good knowledge of what is happening in the business.

POSITION TO INFLUENCE

Choosing where to be so that supervision and influence can be exercised sometimes requires a little skill. Certain people believe that the only place to be is right in the front line whilst others disdain such a hands-on, involved approach because, they argue, it interferes with low-level command. In fact there is no formula saying exactly where leaders should position themselves to control operations. Where that point should be is a personal judgement made at the time and different people will choose different positions.

The boss should not meddle in decisions made by subordinates unless he or she considers that a major error is about to be made. In my view the best way of influencing subordinates is with the lightest touch possible because it is also important not to destroy their confidence or credibility. Sadly, in the Army, I saw the very occasional senior officer who seemed to take a certain pleasure in humiliating subordinates. Personally I feel such bullies, who degrade their position and their people, are the worst kind of leaders. Luckily they are few and far between.

DELEGATION

Sometimes leaders make the mistake of trying to do everything. Those in charge should concentrate on what nobody else is able to do as well. Getting the balance between doing things yourself and delegation is something that can go wrong easily and in some instances I know I have been guilty of this myself.

Shortly after I left the Army I worked with a division of a large company. The divisional director kept his cards very much to his chest and tried to do everything himself. Underneath him his team were all highly intelligent, competent and well motivated. In fact the director was the most intelligent of them all, personable yet slightly remote. He worked far harder than anyone else, had very little free time and looked absolutely exhausted most days. The self-inflicted pressure he was under became so great that he was habitually late for appointments, even with clients, who were not happy to be kept waiting.

The director also knew his job backwards and his failings were from ignorance rather than deliberation or real fault. Previously he had filled a number of very powerful, high-profile appointments where essentially he worked solo. As such he had never really experienced being in a team or how to run one. After a couple of months I suggested to a senior member of the director's team that he raise the matter with the director, which he did. The director listened to what he was told with a wry smile and certain amount of surprise. He realized his colleague was trying to help, readily accepted he was overloaded and that this was probably his own fault. However, he was shocked when told that a couple of the more junior staff interpreted his failure to involve them or delegate work as a lack of trust in them.

That talk did the trick. The director reorganized the division slightly, responsibilities were re-aligned and the team became much more involved. From then onwards the group was far more efficient and effective. The director looked far less tired, and happier too. That senior team member did his director and his company a big service. Of course it does take a man of character and essential decency to take such constructive criticism from his juniors without a certain amount of rancour.

Delegation can also improve morale because it shows a leaders' confidence in the team. But there are some responsibilities that cannot be delegated. In military life these include matters like secret 'eyes only' instructions, confidential reports on key officers, discipline and decisions on who should or should not be promoted. In the commercial world executives may have similar personal responsibilities: confidential board instructions, strategy, appraisals, applying top-level discipline, financial returns and advancement of staff. It is up to leaders everywhere to ensure that they clearly delineate what responsibilities and tasks remain their prerogative so as to avoid any misunderstanding. I think really good leadership involves not only calculated delegation but also helping subordinates to do the job really well.

CHECKING SUBORDINATES

Delegating work most certainly doesn't include ducking responsibility if that delegation doesn't work well or results in things going wrong. The buck still stops on the leader's desk. It is up to leaders to make sure things don't go badly wrong. There are some quite appropriate ways to check on subordinates' activities without discouraging them:

'We seem to have gone wrong somewhere. Can you help me sort it out?'
'Have you any idea how we can avoid this mistake again?'
'I gather things aren't great at the moment. Can I help?'

A leader may not be at fault when things go wrong but that leader should realize just who is responsible for delegated failure.

RAISING STANDARDS

As I have got older and hopefully more mature in judgement I have become increasingly self-critical and try not to delude myself over my own standards and behaviour. I know very well that I often fall short of the principles I set and I blame myself. I suppose, though, that this is better than self-denial or blaming other people for your own mistakes.

Of course leaders should set and maintain standards. But maintaining, developing or creating standards involves everyone, not just the person in charge. Leaders kick-start principles and supervise their practical implementation. But others have to abide by them as well. To this end everyone should be supervised, directly or tacitly, to ensure standards are maintained.

If leaders are poor judges of character they may select entirely the wrong person for a task. This is a serious fault of the person that made the appointment. One way of ensuring that subordinates are up to the job is to train them properly, and a very good way to do this is through personal coaching.

COACHING

When I was managing director of WorldSpace (UK) Limited I visited the company's parent headquarters in Georgetown, Washington DC at least once every two months. During my visits I customarily went to every department in turn to see whether my own operation was performing well enough and how we might improve. During one visit I was with Lemoyne Zacherl, the company's chief financial officer. We discussed accounting methods and the finances involved with the European operation, which I headed. Some of the financial procedures were way above my head, and I admitted as much.

Lemoyne's reaction was utterly decent. 'Well,' he said, 'I don't want people here to know that. As I'm coming to London next week let's spend some time together so I can help you.' Six days later he was in London and he spent four hours coaching me on how I should read and interpret company financial accounts. His instruction was invaluable for me both then and to this day. Lemoyne exhibited real leadership and care – and by coaching improved my performance.

I have also found there is a somewhat surprising personal advantage to coaching as well. Sometimes I have found that sharing my experiences and expertise with other people can help me rethink or clarify my own positions, approach and priorities. Also, if you have done some coaching and explained how you do things to someone who works for you, they are far more likely to do it the way you want without your further involvement. This is exactly the way I trained my officers for Bosnia. Delegation to a well-trained subordinate who you know understands what you require is an easy decision to make.

Figure 10.2 Bosnian Croat militia in 1993

HORSE AND RIDER

The relationship between leaders and the teams they run can be likened to that between a rider and horse. The horse requires control, direction and discipline. Yet it also needs encouragement. The horse is also very well aware if it is being ridden well or badly. It knows instinctively whether its rider is bold or frightened, determined or hesitating. That's not a bad analogy to sum up supervision.

11

Courage and example

THE NATURE OF COURAGE AND EXAMPLE

Army officers are in a martial profession; business executives are not. On military operations the requirement for physical courage is evident and clearly it isn't the same in commerce. The possibility of being killed or having to kill would be a very unusual part of any civilian job specification. But business leaders do sometimes need physical courage; not just in the police, fire service or in jobs where danger is always present such as in the mining or construction industries. Very occasionally executives might require physical daring to deal with events like bank robberies, hostage situations or natural disasters.

The requirement for moral courage is an entirely different and much more common matter. Here the playing field is level, as ethical valour is normally needed at some stage in any job that involves people. Doing the right thing is sometimes very difficult when it would be so much easier to keep your mouth shut or take no action. This less overt courage can sometimes be more difficult than any requirement to be physically brave. So often it is simpler to avoid upsetting the boss, the applecart or angering colleagues than doing or saying what you think to be right.

Courage allows people to meet danger without giving way to fear or intimidation. I emphasise the latter part of this definition as being the heart of it. That inner mental battle to avoid capitulating to fear or intimidation is at the core of being courageous. I remember seeing a service charity advertisement on the front page of a national news-paper, which featured a photograph of an old soldier. Underneath were words to this effect: 'Tiny, awarded the Distinguished Conduct Medal twice, was once so brave he didn't know what fear was. Now he is scared of a mouse.' Whoever wrote those words missed the point entirely. Courage is not the absence of fear; it is its control. If you have no fear then courage doesn't come into it.

I link courage with example in this chapter because they are inter-twined. In the armed forces courage under fire is obviously an example to others. But this is reflected in business too. It takes moral courage to swim against the tide of popular opinion or be the person who dis-agrees on principle or for ethical reasons. That is an example to others. It takes courage to face a hostile interviewer on television as an exec-utive or spokesman for a company that is under real pressure. That too is an example for others. Even leading a pitch to a potential client can involve more than just a few nerves. Sometimes that new business may be vital to the continuation of not just one job but many. How you lead under such pressure demonstrates considerable example.

Courage is like the tide; it can be high and it can be low. Speaking from my own experience I know that my ability to control fears and anxieties is better at some times than others. Lord Moran, Winston Churchill's doctor, who wrote a book called *The Anatomy of Courage*, believed that each person had a store of bravery and when that stock was exhausted, that was it. I do not know whether he was right or wrong. But it seems to me that at least some ability to display courage and endure can be refreshed or replenished by altered circumstances – such as a break or a holiday. This is one of the main reasons why the Army insists that soldiers on operations have short so-called 'rest and relaxation' (R&R) leave periods halfway through six-month tours of duty.

For me, leading by example also meant a deliberate decision to be in front whenever possible. One night in Bosnia, when things were pretty grim, I overheard a conversation between a non-commissioned officer and a newly arrived soldier. I was alone, sitting drinking a coffee in a blacked-out corridor (there had been a power cut). Then two soldiers came out of their accommodation and lit up cigarettes some 25 feet from me. They had no idea I was there and I kept quiet. The conversation went something like this:

'I've seen the bloody commanding officer on the news in the UK but not since I've been here', said one, clearly newly arrived.

The other, obviously an older soldier, asked, 'Have you been under fire yet?'

'No.'

'Well when you are, look in front and you'll see Colonel Bob!'

Until that moment I was absolutely exhausted and very low but when I heard that I could have floated off the ammunition tin on which I was sitting.

COURAGE: THE BUSINESS QUALITY

Moral courage, and occasionally physical bravery too, are certainly business leadership requirements. Executives often have to take risks and sometimes make very difficult decisions. Aristotle, the Greek philosopher, maintained that courage was the primary human virtue. So it is in business too. Courage is the bedrock for integrity, accountability, robustness and the desire to succeed. The writer J K Rowling puts it succinctly: 'Anything's possible if you've got enough nerve', and in this sense nerve is synonymous with courage.

Let me highlight a few business practices which I think involve courage to a lesser or greater extent. In business some form of courage may be required when:

- deciding to say what you really think when everyone else is going for an easy option that you firmly believe to be wrong;
- trusting colleagues to do what they are meant to do – when you feel you could do it so much better;
- being prepared to make decisions when the situation is uncertain and the risks considerable;
- admitting that you have made a mistake or got things wrong;
- accepting you do not have a complete solution and need some help;
- sharing facts and details with colleagues from other parts of the company who might take credit that rightly belongs to you;
- taking a detailed and analytical approach to a problem to ensure it is right when everyone else is telling you to hurry up;

- standing up for yourself or colleagues when you or they are being bullied or intimidated by a forceful boss or colleague;
- being unprepared to accept the opinion of others when you feel deeply that they are wrong;
- accepting that you are not up to the task in hand and need to learn how to do something;
- understanding that the team is working wrongly and setting out a new course when so much effort has already been put into the old (failed) approach;
- accepting or giving out feedback which implicitly criticizes your own work;
- being prepared to deal with new problems rather than just shelving or avoiding them;
- accepting that others have worked really hard – perhaps harder than you yourself;
- giving generous credit to a colleague who has achieved much more than yourself;
- putting the needs of your client well before your own convenience;
- apologizing!
- keeping going because you know that is right despite the attractions of giving up;
- going on 'gut' reaction when you feel that normal logic gives incorrect solutions;
- altering the way things have always been done because you feel that is right even if unpopular;
- having a totally honest approach to everyone and every problem;
- being yourself rather than adopting some corporate company image.

COURAGEOUS EXAMPLE

After the Army General Bill Slim made a serious name for himself in civilian life as an expert on leadership. Once, when being questioned by business executives on how they might stimulate courage and integrity in business, he answered quite simply: 'By example.'

Of course I am biased, but my father was a huge inspiration and example to me. In the Second World War he had been a signaller in Bomber Command but after hostilities ended he had remained in uniform as an RAF Regiment officer. By the mid-1950s he was a squadron leader on secondment with the Aden Protectorate Levies (APL) in what is now Yemen. My mother, brother, sister and I accompanied him and lived in an officer's quarter in Aden. But for most of the time he was up-country on operations.

On 15 June 1955 my father was second in command of a convoy of vehicles tasked to reach Fort Rabat, isolated and surrounded by rebel fighters led by a man called Salem Ali Mawer. About one hundred APL personnel, mounted in three Land Rovers and nine lorries, moved into Wadi Hatib, the only route to Fort Rabat. The wadi's sides ranged up to 9,000 feet in some parts. It was desolate and very hot country in all senses. Despite a little sniping the convoy managed to get all the way to Fort Rabat. It delivered its supplies and relieved those men due for rotation. Then at 1.30 pm it began the return run. But by then Salem Ali Mawer was ready and waiting.

Within a few minutes the force was being heavily engaged from the mountainous slopes surrounding it. Almost immediately a young British officer and an Arab soldier were killed. Several others were wounded. Wing Commander Rodney Marshall, the commanding officer, ordered my father to evacuate the wounded to a safer place about one mile further down Wadi Hatib. Under intense fire he managed to do this but then, from some retreating soldiers, he learned that Rodney Marshall had been killed. To make matters worse, the senior Arab officer was also dead. In fact there were no officers left alive with the main body of the convoy. The escaping soldiers told Dad that all was lost and that nothing further could be done. My father obviously did not agree. I quote from an official report of what happened next:

Squadron Leader Stewart assumed command of the Force and immediately organized a volunteer party. He led them back into the ambush area which was under heavy and accurate fire, in an attempt to recover the dead bodies and wounded. Unable to locate the body of the Wing Commander he recovered a three ton vehicle which contained a dead guard and had one tyre deflated by rifle fire. He personally drove the damaged truck back under fire, twice stopping to pick up wounded. More casualties were inflicted during the return passage through the Wadi. In all there were eight killed and seven wounded. Having assumed command of the Force he moved it tactically to an emergency airstrip and organized the evacuation of the most seriously wounded. Sniping ensued during this evacuation and hostile and accurate fire was encountered.

I took that quotation from my father's citation for the Military Cross in the *London Gazette*. He clearly led by example, and so it wasn't just me he inspired. When my father died, very young at 52, his driver from years before travelled right across the country to be there. Dad would have been pleased.

Figure 11.1 Myself with Dad and brother Andrew after Dad received the MC in 1955

Twelve years after that ambush in Aden, my father took me to RMA Sandhurst to begin my officer training. It was obvious to him that I was nervous and very apprehensive – to me the instructors looked so impressive and I felt so immature. Just before he left me on Sandhurst's Grand Entrance steps he turned to me and said, 'Robert, don't worry. Even the Queen gets diarrhoea. And always look downwards before looking upwards.' I knew what he meant. Never be over-impressed by anyone and always care about those for whom you have responsibility as your first priority.

On 26 December 1992 Lieutenant Justin Freeland, from B Squadron 9th/12th Lancers under my operational control, was taking part in a line-crossing operation to bring UN supplies into Northern Bosnia. He was commanding his troop of four Scimitar vehicles in the area east of Tuzla. Suddenly three mortar rounds fired by the Bosnian Serb Army opposite landed amongst his vehicles. A piece of shrapnel went straight through Justin's upper left arm.

Justin's radio message about what happened was priceless. He spoke slowly, calmly, deliberately and in his normal voice, despite being in obvious pain. I remember the gist of his words as: 'All OK. I've been hit. It's gone through. Carrying on.' That radio message was heard by everyone listening to the battalion radio net. We were all deeply impressed. It was a classic example of how a young officer should behave, and he set a very high example. It also demonstrated where officers should position themselves under fire – right in front of their troops!

The injury was not slight, and Justin had to undergo an operation by our field surgical team. I was waiting outside the operating theatre when the surgeon cleaned the wound by pushing a large needle from one side of his arm to the other. Two days later he was evacuated for full medical treatment in the United Kingdom. I am sure that his father, the late General Sir Ian Freeland, who had been my General Officer Commanding in Northern Ireland when I was a platoon commander in Londonderry 22 years before, would have been very proud of his son.

Can anyone doubt that leaders need to set an example? 'Do as I do' is obviously a far more powerful directive than 'do as I say – but don't do'. Little actions can be catalytic in effect. On occasion in Bosnia I would wander around my base very late at night visiting sentry positions. Observation duty between 2–4 am is probably the worst task ever; you cannot get decent sleep before or after the duty. Sentries are always posted in pairs at night and so sometimes I would stand one of the men down and take his place. I knew that such small gestures were very well received, because invariably the next day RSM Charlie Stephens would mention he knew I had done it. Clearly the word had spread through the ranks that the commanding officer was not above doing a bit of 'porridge'.

BUSINESS CONTEXT

Translated into commercial life, there are numerous parallels of good example. Little gestures like bosses selling at a counter, standing on a stall in an exhibition or taking a turn at dealing with customer complaints are all noticed and have effect. Being an example essentially means never asking others to do what you would not. Human beings are very quick to notice if you do not practise what you preach. For example, if you are keen that your staff receive formal training, attend a course yourself explaining that you too need to get better at your job as well.

When I was part of the teams preparing bids for new business in Hill and Knowlton the work normally extended well past the end of the working day. Quite often the bid team had to stay at work long into the evening to get things right. Preparing new business bids is never an easy ride. But I noticed that one particular senior executive in the company always remained behind in his office when we did this. Often he would join us doing whatever needed to be done, regardless of the simplicity of the task. He was quite prepared to assemble folders or photocopy documents, which his personal assistant would have done for him during normal working hours. That senior executive truly understood the motivation of good example.

THE CHIEF OPERATING OFFICER

For three years I was managing director of WorldSpace (UK) Limited, based in London and responsible for operations in Europe. The company was the world's first international digital satellite radio broadcaster. A few months after I arrived a new chief operating officer was appointed to the parent company based in Washington, USA. His name was Rod Puleo.

Within a week or so of assuming his appointment Rod was visiting the company's foreign stations and being briefed. I spent two hours talking to him about what we were doing and how we were planning for the future. Rod was very friendly, supportive and efficient. During his visit he spent at least a third of his time meeting, talking and working with employees at their place of work. He asked everyone who they were and what they did, and remembered their names.

Six months or so after Rod arrived I had a good opportunity to see Rod perform under real pressure. I received a phone call from him. He was in Johannesburg at the company's office there. He told me that he would like some help to launch a company product throughout Africa. Rod asked if I could get there to assist him. I was flattered that he had asked for my help. In addition, I thought my Director of Business Development, Atef Awad, would also be a great assistance so we both flew to South Africa the next day.

Rod Puleo had arrived in South Africa with the intention of leading the product launch, which he felt had been going off the rails. As the company's chief operating officer he believed he had to step in and take responsibility for sorting the matter out. He had also spent a little time visiting the shop floor. When he was with one group of people he grew seriously concerned. They all knew him from previous visits, clearly respecting and liking him. They showed little respect for the way they were led by the company's local executives who, they suggested, were simply out for all they could grab. Two of them, who had been with the company for a while, mentioned that often they felt they were not actually working for the company but some other entity. They implied that at least part of the management was 'moonlighting' – running a private business with company assets. Rod's suspicions were aroused.

My visit with Atef Awad was perfectly standard operational practice as we were needed to help with the launch. But now Rod asked us also to keep our eyes and ears open for any indications of serious irregularities. We did so, and turned up a few disturbing facts, which we reported directly and only to Rod.

Despite his worries, Rod led and organized the product launch superbly. He seemed like a one-man activity centre, bursting with new initiatives. His energy radiated out to everyone who worked with him.

Whilst Atef and I helped with the business of the launch we also assisted Rod privately to investigate what else was happening. It didn't take long for us to spot that a great deal was wrong. Most importantly there seemed to be a number of financial irregularities, with monies being paid to other companies for no reason. I will not say any more on this, suffice to say that in the end the matter finished with some executives in court and a new management structure in place.

Rod Puleo illustrated exactly how a top executive should behave. Radiating optimism and calm, he inspired everyone by his demeanour. Nobody wanted to let him down. Colleagues throughout the company respected and admired him for his hard work, decency and integrity. His mind was always turning over new ways to do our business and he encouraged others to think like that too. Very impressively, he remembered everyone's name no matter how obscure their job!

Rod Puleo was a top executive with huge moral courage and integrity. He also fully understood the need for him to lead by example and, by so doing, turned around a failing product launch and probably saved the South African division of the company from implosion.

LEONIDAS: ULTIMATE COURAGE AND EXAMPLE

Leadership really counts when the chips are down. Staying calm and in control during crisis situations is where leaders really show their mettle. It was Robert Louis Stephenson who once advised, 'Keep your fears to yourself and share your courage with others.' For me perhaps the greatest historic example of raw courage occurred at the Pass of Thermopylae in Greece during August 480 BC.

King Leonidas of Sparta, together with 300 of his personal bodyguard, 900 Helots and 700 Thespians, established a defensive blocking position in the Pass of Thermopylae. His mission was to stop the invasion of Greece by Persian King Xerxes whose army numbered at least 80,000.

For two days Leonidas held the pass, fighting in the front line and killing 20,000 enemy troops. Well before he took up his defensive position Leonidas knew his fate was sealed. Yet he was prepared to sacrifice himself and all those who remained voluntarily with him to gain time for others in Greece to organize their defences. Leonidas and his 300 Spartans knew that they would die and they did so willingly to save others. It was cold-blooded courage and extreme leadership by total example.

I have visited the monument to Leonidas at the site of the battle. Today the battlefield remains largely as it was almost 2,500 years ago. The monument is a bronze statue of the King. A sign, under the statue, reads simply: 'Μολών λαβέ' ('Come and get them!') which the Spartans reputedly shouted when the Persians asked them to put down their weapons before they were finally slaughtered. If that was put in modern parlance it might also read: 'Bring it on'.

12

Negotiation

BAPTISM OF FIRE

Everyone negotiates, one way or another. Negotiation is a perfectly normal part of all human activities at home and at work. In commercial life negotiation with groups like customers, trade unions, suppliers, investors and banks is an entirely routine part of life too. But when problems crop up they need to be sorted out as soon as possible. Ignoring the need to negotiate is usually unwise.

I experienced my first taste of serious negotiation at 42 years old. Suddenly I was confronted by the absolute need to negotiate solutions or risk my mission failing in Bosnia. I was never taught much about negotiation in the Army; not at Sandhurst, two staff colleges or on any course I attended. But luckily I had studied the subject during my time at university. Some of that academic stuff stuck and I was grateful to clutch at it. But my practical learning curve was steep and on the job. It started on 20 October 1992.

Brigadier Andrew Cumming, later to command all British soldiers in the Balkans, and I had arranged to meet Tihomir Blaskic, the Bosnian Croat commander, at his headquarters, the Hotel Vitez. Our reconnaissance party had spent the night at our base a couple of miles away. As we drove into Vitez at 9 am we were stopped by a Bosnian Croat roadblock. It looked like we would not be allowed to pass, so both Andrew and I got out of the vehicles.

We weren't sure how to act, so tackled the situation head-on. 'You have no right to stop us. Get the barricade open now. Don't argue with us, we are UN officers.' Our somewhat robust approach worked, and the soldiers let us through.

It was worryingly quiet on the Vitez streets. We felt something must be wrong, especially when shooting broke out as we approached the hotel. Jumping out of our Land Rovers we took cover and cocked our weapons. After a minute or so the firing stopped. Some nearby Bosnian Croat soldiers told us they had been shooting at some Bosnian Muslims and not at us. We went into the hotel but Blaskic was not there. A man called Mario Cerkez, explained that Blaskic was in Novi Travnik, where serious fighting between Bosnian Croats and Bosnian Muslims had apparently erupted overnight. We could certainly hear shooting and explosions some miles away.

We knew that if we didn't secure some form of ceasefire our chances of getting soldiers into Central Bosnia were probably at an end. The MoD had told us that the deployment would not occur if fighting were taking place between so-called allies. We both felt we had no choice but to try and stop it.

We told Cerkez that we expected his side to stop fighting, and we would insist the Bosnian Muslims did the same. In addition we asked him to ensure that we would be able to pass through any of his road-blocks throughout the area. He said he would try to arrange it, provided the Bosnian Muslims reciprocated.

Andrew and I decided I should find the Bosnian Muslim commander and would go with just Captain Nick Stansfield, our military inter-preter. I asked Cerkez to point us in the right direction and a man called Zelko climbed aboard my Land Rover. He directed us as we drove across town. After a few minutes we arrived at what looked like a school, with every window in the building blown out. At the build-ing's entrance we met a couple of Bosnian Muslim soldiers and asked to see their commander. They seemed to know Zelko, and were not in the slightest bit aggressive towards him. Bosnia was so weird; a Kafka novel brought to life!

Upstairs in an office was a thick-set man with a large moustache. He introduced himself as Dzidic Sefkija and said he was in command. Indicating all the broken glass around his desk he told me he was lucky to be alive as an anti-tank missile had been launched at his office during the night, breaking the building's windows.

I asked him to stop fighting. Angrily he declined. He also refused to take his roadblocks down, because he said that a force of Bosnian

Croats would then be able to get through to Novi Travnik. He felt they would reinforce other Bosnian Croats who, he said, were attacking Muslims there. I argued with him but he adamantly refused to budge. In the end I asked if he could warn his people in Novi Travnik that I was going to try to get to see them.

It seemed sensible for me to try to get a safe passage for this so I asked him to arrange one for us at 3 pm. This he agreed to do. I was just finishing with Sefkija when his phone rang. He handed me the receiver. I was a bit shocked; the call was for me!

On the phone was Dan Damon of SKY News. Goodness knows how he discovered where I was. He said he had been ambushed and was sheltering in a house by a Bosnian Muslim roadblock because firing was still occurring. Could I rescue him, he asked? To be honest I had other priorities but I said I would try, especially as his position was on our route back to our base.

Together with Zelko we drove back to Hotel Vitez where we re-joined Andrew Cumming. I briefed Andrew on what had happened. Back with Cerkez again we asked him to warn the Bosnian Croats in Novi Travnik that they should expect a convoy of UN vehicles at about 3 pm. He agreed, but said stopping the fighting would be very difficult as the Bosnian Muslims had taken hostages.

We started to drive back to our base, and en route drew up where we thought Dan Damon was holed up near a checkpoint. As we stopped, Dan and his wife Siân, who filmed his reports, emerged from a house. Dan told us that his Lada vehicle had been hit by two shots that went straight through the car.

But the Bosnian Muslims at the checkpoint refused to allow us through. Their commander was a huge man who spoke little English. I had no idea what to do but decided to just shout loudly – the stereo-typed British way with foreigners! I demanded that the man remove his mines and a bus blocking our way immediately. My negotiation tactics were rough and ready but, with a slightly mocking smile, the giant agreed. By around midday we were back at our base with Dan and Siân Damon and their 'wounded' Lada.

All round the base, a school soon to become our headquarters, there was intense small arms shooting. An anti-aircraft gun, only 200 metres from us, was also firing at targets we couldn't see. All hell seemed to have been let loose. As we were parking up some Bosnian Croat soldiers in black uniforms tried to occupy the school. Apprehensively I approached them, wondering what they would make of me. Pointing at the UN flag I told them to get out – no negotiation this time – and that is exactly what they did.

At 2.30 pm our small convoy of vehicles left to go to Novi Travnik, and 15 minutes later we were at a crossroads, also a Bosnian Croat checkpoint, about a mile outside the town. There we said goodbye to the SKY team as they took a route back to the coast in their patched-up vehicle.

My aim was to get into Novi Travnik, find the various commanders and convince them to stop fighting. Looking back at it now I was pretty naive to think it would be that simple. At 3 pm we listened carefully at the crossroads and heard no firing. Perhaps, we thought, the ceasefire was implemented.

I led four vehicles as we left the checkpoint behind and steered directly into Novi Travnik. Nick Stansfield was driving. The town seemed absolutely still. I took my radio headphones off so that I could hear as much as possible. Nobody was on the streets. I wasn't even sure where the centre of town was but supposed this route led there. I had no idea where to find the local headquarters and simply hoped for the best.

Suddenly there was huge noise – from all sides. Firing had erupted from the modern flats and houses lining both sides of the street. The noise was terrifying and bullets seemed to be going everywhere. We were in the middle. I saw a burst hit the concrete on my left. I had led the convoy right into a killing area and the shooting seemed to be right at us. My shoulders curved in towards themselves, maybe to make myself less of a target. I was terrified. 'Keep going Nick,' was all I could mumble.

Automatic fire and perhaps an anti-tank rocket splashed over the buildings to our right and then left too. There was no time for anything but getting through it. My own Land Rover seemed to be through the worst but what about the others? Leaning forward and looking sideways into the passenger-door mirror I could see the next two vehicles following. Maybe we had all made it.

Screeching around the streets as we attempted to get well clear of the shooting, I suddenly saw a man waving crazily at us. We stopped and he directed us into a side street. We drove in and found another man. I noticed the second soldier's uniform carried Bosnian Muslim badges.

His commander's office was apparently on the second floor. Andrew Cumming, Nick and I entered the headquarters, leaving the rest of our party to go to ground and seek protection where they could. I hoped they would be safe.

'Lendo', was the only word the rather surly Bosnian Muslim commander used when he stuck out his hand. We introduced ourselves and immediately asked him to stop fighting and, if he had hostages, to give them to us. Lendo said a ceasefire was impossible and so too was any hostage release. 'Anyway, what power do you have with so few people and a handful of vehicles in the middle of all this carnage?' he asked. He had a point. Then after a few minutes he suddenly announced that we could take away one hostage.

A man was hauled into the room. He looked terrified; his eyes were frantic. I suppose he must have thought he was going to be murdered. His name was Illya. I tried to reassure him. After telling Lendo that we were determined to negotiate a ceasefire, we left, taking Illya with us. Outside the firing had continued sporadically.

Using Illya as a guide we drove back across Novi Travnik. We arrived at a restaurant, dubbed the Café Grand, and there in a bar we met the Bosnian Croat local commander named Dario Kordich. Thin, with a crew cut and over-large glasses, he shouted rather than spoke. Around him were a group of other men, presumably officers. We told Kordich that we hoped to negotiate a ceasefire. I indicated Illya, saying rather proudly that we had rescued him. But Kordich couldn't seem to care less. He said Lendo was a war criminal and asked what we could do to get him arrested.

Kordich said that 14 Bosnian Croats were dead already. He blamed Lendo, who he thought to be personally responsible and refused to even talk to him. But, he said, he would be prepared to speak with another Bosnian Muslim commander called Dzemal Merdan. How can we arrange that, we asked? Kordich produced a mobile phone, which really surprised us as we had been told by the MoD's intelligence staff in London that such phones simply didn't work in Bosnia.

Within a minute or so Merdan was on the phone. He agreed that a ceasefire was possible and he would fax an agreement to meet through to the Café Grand. A few minutes later a fax arrived. I was staggered – first a working mobile phone and then ceasefires arranged by fax. This was unlike anything I had envisaged.

Andrew Cumming and I agreed that we would chair any ceasefire negotiations and the Bosnian Croats insisted that Merdan be present. Over the phone we agreed with Merdan that I would drive to Zenica to fetch him, and would take him back after the negotiation. We had done everything we could for the moment and so returned to our base at the school. Thankfully no one shot at us as we did so.

Later I went with my driver to pick up Merdan. There and back should have taken two hours or so. En route, and in total darkness, we suddenly came across a deserted roadblock with mines around the barricades. I moved them very carefully, fully aware that, if they had armed tilt switches it would be over for me. But my luck held and eventually we collected Merdan in Zenica and returned to Hotel Vitez where, at last, I found Tihomir Blaskic.

We all sat in easy chairs in Blaskic's office, but frankly I had no idea how to convince both sides to stop fighting. At one stage Blaskic suggested that I was probably pro-Bosnian Muslim and anti-Bosnian Croat. That really made me angry and I quite forcefully rebutted him. Blaskic withdrew the comment.

Repeatedly I asked both Blaskic and Merdan to order a ceasefire but Blaskic refused point blank unless Lendo surrendered to him. For his part Merdan was quite prepared to sign an immediate cessation of hostilities. Both Merdan and Blaskic had been good friends in the Yugoslav National Army before the war and seemed on good terms still. Our discussions dragged on until about 3 am the next morning but we still couldn't get a ceasefire. Once or twice we were asked whether we had enough soldiers on the ground to supervise any potential ceasefire agreements. Of course we didn't, we were simple a reconnaissance party. I simply said we would do everything we could to help.

I returned to our base, shattered, and fell asleep on the floor in the gymnasium immediately. My baptism of negotiation fire had involved six fraught meetings within a day and had been a huge learning curve. In the end a ceasefire was agreed a couple of weeks later. It was organized by Captain Simon Ellis, my operations officer, whilst I was back in Germany. Like me it was his first experience of negotiating but his persistence in the end achieved what was needed. Because of Simon's work the fighting was stopped and my battalion was able to deploy into Central Bosnia.

ON-THE-JOB LESSONS

That day, 20 October 1992, was probably the longest day of my life and I certainly learnt a few lessons on negotiation that day:

- Have a plan. I knew what I wanted but had no real idea how to achieve it. That should not happen. From then on I had to have a negotiation plan in advance if at all possible.
- Know the situation. I had no real idea of the situation before I launched headlong into it. That was a huge mistake, which had to be avoided in future. I was lucky nobody was killed or wounded

– particularly in the ambush we drove through as we approached Novi Travnik.

■ Up-front leadership can work. Acting like a warlord, with a forceful and robust approach, got us through a couple of roadblocks. Sometimes up-front leadership, taking charge of a situation, is best. I was to use that lesson repeatedly for the rest of my time in Bosnia.

■ Know the participants in advance. Arriving at an unknown place and walking in cold to meet a group of people I had never met before was hardly conducive to success. It was very important to get to know those who would be negotiating. From their point of view they would be far more likely to trust a negotiator they knew. From then onwards I always tried to meet and talk with all sides before calling them to a negotiation.

■ Negotiate in one place. Running between negotiating parties was difficult, and should be avoided. It would have been far better to get all sides together in the same place where I had control of both the negotiation agenda and the environment.

■ Bring something to the table. Negotiating without something to offer – like troops able to supervise a potential ceasefire – was not the way. In future I ought to bring something to the negotiating table of some value.

■ Have instant communications with all parties. Good communications are essential during negotiations. If people weren't all together in one place then I would make sure I could speak with them very quickly.

■ Know your own no-go areas. I knew instinctively that which I would not tolerate. Bosnian Croat soldiers deploying into our base was simply unacceptable. Being accused of being pro-Bosnian Muslim by Blaskic required a strong riposte and I gave it there and then.

■ Why not try for the impossible? Ask the impossible and maybe, just maybe, something good may come of it. We managed to secure the release of one hostage by this tactic.

■ Write things down. Writing down the issues that need to be discussed is well worth the effort as it creates something tangible that can be reviewed and amended. In Bosnia the various sides loved paperwork and it always impressed them. From then onwards I always tried to draft a discussion document, which I hoped would end up as an agreement.

■ Keep going. Finally, I learnt that in negotiation defeat should not be an option. We had to keep going even when it seemed impossible. I passed on the negotiation process to Simon Ellis because I had to return to Germany. Simon achieved a ceasefire 14 days later by just keeping going at it.

NEGOTIATION BASICS

Planning

The first step of any intended activity is to decide what you wish to achieve. Negotiation is no different and should be carefully planned. But in Bosnia I was frequently presented with a situation where negotiation was needed at almost no notice. Anything that could help me under such pressure was useful. To that end I always carried the four headings of the negotiation template – Aim, Strength, Weakness, Approach – around with me in my Filofax (see Figure 2.8).

After 20 October 1992 I also decided to produce my own one-pager on negotiation, which I issued to all officers, warrant officers and non-commissioned officers in my battalion (Figure 12.1).

Place and time

Organizing a decent, appropriate place for negotiations and fixing exactly when they are to happen are standard prerequisites. I normally used my headquarters or a company base for most negotiations I chaired in Bosnia because they were considered neutral locations and I could ensure I set up the meeting room to my liking.

Compromise

A successful negotiation normally requires compromise from all sides. The negotiator has to find a solution that all participants can live with. Ideally everyone should also feel that any compromise they agree brings benefits of equal or greater advantage to themselves. In Bosnia my initial approach was invariably to say that nobody wanted war so we should all aim to stop it. No participant could possibly disagree with that so at least we started with one agreed statement!

---

1 CHESHIRE GP
NEGOTIATION
To be carried by all officers, warrant officers and NCOs

Authority

We act under UN Security Council Resolution 770 (13 Aug 92) which authorises the use of 'all measures necessary' to ensure the safe passage of humanitarian aid.

Under the Geneva Conventions active hostilities must not be carried out against civilians. To do so is a war crime.

Preparation

Before starting any negotiation understand the situation as far as is possible.

Prepare a negotiation plan.

Meet participants in advance (if possible) and try to get their trust.

Approach

Know exactly what you hope to achieve.

Take command of the negotiation from the start.

Be neutral, straight and honest.

Record

Try to get agreements reached in writing with all sides signing.

Report any agreements reached quickly – if necessary by radio.

Vitez   Lt Col R A Stewart
20 Nov 92

Figure 12.1 Negotiation one-pager

Personal style

I cannot stress enough just how important the style and approach of a negotiator is to ultimate success. Obviously the negotiator must stay in control and equally he or she should project an image of confidence, unflappability, determination, knowledge and concern to be fair to everyone. Not only must negotiator(s) be impartial but they must be seen to be consistently so at all times, including outside the actual negotiations themselves.

The vast majority of my negotiations in Bosnia were to try and arrange ceasefires and sometimes they went on for days and days. But at every one of them almost without exception participants suggested that I was favouring their opponents. My standard response to such an accusation was to smile politely and say that, as I had been shot at by every side present at the negotiation I was truly neutral. The comment almost always raised a smile.

Respect

Unless participants have respect for the negotiator they are unlikely to accept his or her adjudication. In Bosnia I was sometimes asked by European Community Monitoring Mission officers to chair negotiations that they had set up because the participants said they would only sit down to negotiate if 'Colonel Stewart' was in the chair. Whilst this was flattering it was extremely time-consuming and somewhat irritating when I had so much else to do. It did, however, imply that I had developed a reputation for fairness, which is terribly important in negotiations.

Know the participants

It is very difficult to negotiate between parties you do not know. I learnt this on 20 October 1992 and it stood me in good stead thereafter. Getting to know belligerent commanders was the main reason why I held dinner nights at my base in Vitez. Once we managed to get a Danish soldier, who was being held as a hostage by the Bosnian Croats, released when the formal UN team had had no luck. The commander who authorized the soldiers' release had joined my officers and me for dinner a few nights before. He released the hostage soldier with the message back to me that he had really appreciated our hospitality. Maybe the returned Dane was a 'thank you' letter!

On 3 March 1993 I was chairing a ceasefire meeting at which high-level Bosnian Croat and Bosnian Muslim commanders together with government representatives were due to be present. I had despatched a second lieutenant to pick up one key participant, a Bosnian Muslim corps commander, from miles away. He arrived at the rendezvous in a rush, saw what he thought to be the officer and bundled him into the back of his Warrior before travelling quickly back to my headquarters. It was only when I was chairing the meeting that we discovered the man sitting in the corps commander's chair was actually the headquarters' cleaner. It was not funny at the time.

The process

Normally, whenever I conducted a negotiation I tried to follow a set format:

- Welcome participants and explain the reason for the meeting.
- Present an assessment of the situation as I see it.
- Ask if everyone wants to reach an agreement.
- Ask participants to state where they stand.
- Identify what participants would not negotiate.
- Establish and agree common ground.
- Return to difficult areas. Listen carefully and suggest/discuss options.
- Keep pressure up to get agreement.
- Maintain a record, and start a draft agreement as soon as possible.
- If agreement is reached, get it signed there and then.
- Devise a means of monitoring compliance.
- Report results to higher command as soon as possible.

Compliance

Although everyone may act in good faith when they sign an agreement, things often change later and very quickly too, particularly in Bosnia where chains of command were transitory. Writing compliance checks into any agreement makes sense and I always tried to do it.

The media

In my experience the media can often be far more powerful than a gun. Journalists can have a direct and positive role too, provided they are happy to play a part – which they normally were for us as we were neutral. Speaking into a camera and saying that it can be a war crime to deprive women and children of food, clothing and medicines right in front of a roadblock prior to asking its commander to state his name, rank and why he is not prepared to let humanitarian aid pass can be a powerful tool to achieve a resolution. On two occasions I negotiated just like that, with a camera. Both times it worked and the roadblock was immediately opened for UN traffic.

The media are important in other, less direct, ways too. First, it can make reports about the meeting, thereby building up public profile and raising expectations that some progress might result. That alone can induce greater flexibility amongst participants. Second, throughout negotiations such pressure builds if reporters continue to badger participants. Finally, reports of a successful negotiation in the media might also buttress the requirement for participants to comply properly. If compliance does not happen then the media can be used to highlight this fact and focus attention on those who are guilty.

Walk-out tactics

In one ceasefire negotiation I was so utterly fed up and irritated with the lack of progress and how much of my time it was taking up, I decided I could do no more. As one side was skirting round the issues for the umpteenth time I interrupted and announced that it was clear to me that I was wasting my time trying to get two intransigent sides to agree to stop killing one another. I announced that I was leaving because I had other urgent matters requiring my attention. I packed my notes up into a briefcase and stood up to go. As I did so I noticed that each side looked a bit alarmed. Then one said that they would prefer I stayed. The other side said the same. Suddenly I realized I did have something with which to bargain; I had my presence! That cheered me a little. With some (pretended) reluctance I was convinced to stay and we reached agreement on a ceasefire an hour later.

NEGOTIATION – WHAT A LEADER DOES

Problem solving by negotiation is a core function for anyone in charge of any enterprise. Sometimes just having the boss in charge of negotiations was a fillip to resolution. In Bosnia it was frequently essential that I led operations like ceasefire negotiations and line crossings, because belligerent commanders expected me to do so.

In business, who does the negotiations is a crucial decision for leaders. Unlike the military, it is rare for the top leaders to get involved in the nitty-gritty of commercial negotiation sessions. This is sensible. But top business leaders most definitely should be intimately involved in what is happening, albeit from a slight distance.

A leader should be the court of last resort for difficulties that cannot be solved elsewhere. After all, if the top person cannot sort out a problem, there aren't many other places to go, are there?

13

Communication

SPEAKING, WRITING AND LISTENING

'Look downwards before you look upwards' my father had advised when I arrived at Sandhurst in 1967. His meaning was clear. Care about those who work for you before you concern yourself with pleasing superiors. The way you look after those that work for you depends a lot on communication. Talking and writing are the primary, although not the only, means to do this. Sometimes the best way of communicating is by demonstrating what you mean by action on the ground. In Bosnia I always did what I said I would do. If I had promised that my soldiers would be positioned at a certain point by a specific time I ensured that happened.

Communication is very much a two-way matter. Listening to soldiers, employees, customers, stakeholders and the like is something a leader must do well. The Army is a hierarchical organization and instructions go downwards through a well-established chain of command. It is a formal, proven means of passing instructions along. But it doesn't necessarily result in perfect understanding as information gets filtered through various levels.

Confirmation that the message has been passed and interpreted correctly is always necessary because instructions can be corrupted during their passage, normally by simple mistake rather than malign intention. I always took steps to see whether those at the end of the chain did indeed understand what was happening, by asking them. This may appear slightly disloyal to intermediate commanders or managers but it is a leader's responsibility to make sure things happen. A few ruffled feathers may be the price paid to ensure that everyone truly understands and accepts what they have to do. It also ensures that intermediates try hard to pass on instructions accurately.

Commercial companies normally have a far flatter hierarchy than the Army, and it is usually not so rigid. In my experience, a chief executive officer informally asking an employee what he or she thinks of something being proposed or implemented is not normally seen as any form of disloyalty or checking on intermediate managers.

PUBLIC SPEAKING

I have listened to a great number of speeches over the years. A few have been brilliant, most reasonable, and others not so good, whilst some have been appalling. The ability to communicate well in public is a crucial requirement for a leader. Most people would accept that Margaret Thatcher and Tony Blair were very good public speakers and also adept at repartee. On the other hand, Gordon Brown often looks uncomfortable in public and is not good at putting over his point of view publicly.

Mindful that I could be better too, I make the following observations about public speaking:

- Decide exactly what you want to achieve in your speech. As you think about what you are going to say ask yourself all the time whether your words support the aim. Think back to recent speeches you have heard and try to recall what was in them. If you can recall two points made by the speaker, whoever it was has done very well indeed. Any speaker is lucky if people remember two points from their speech 10 minutes after it. So decide what particular messages are vital and make sure that these are remembered!
- Most people have difficulty listening carefully for more than 20 minutes. I need to take notes and refer back to them if I really want to remember in detail what has been said. For me, 20 minutes or less is a good yardstick for the maximum length of any speech or address.
- The most effective way of speaking is to talk to people rather than hector or lecture them. If there is a big crowd of people and you feel you might have to shout at them to be heard then perhaps it might

be wise to use a microphone. Microphones are aids not crutches. Do not think that their use implies you haven't got a strong enough voice. The way you say it and what you say are far more important than the volume you use.

■ Use plain language that is readily understood. Recently I listened to a brilliant man whose knowledge on his subject was immense but he quickly lost myself and everyone else present by using difficult words and convoluted ideas. He talked for half an hour but very few people were listening to what he said beyond the first few minutes.

■ Whatever you say should be appropriate. I remember one Army general who spoke to the officers in my battalion. He spoke clearly and well. Enthusiastically he told us all about the latest bureaucratic reorganization in the MoD. But what he was talking about was of no interest to a unit that was in the front line. Everyone wants to hear about matters of concern to them.

■ Sometimes using a gimmick may work well. I have seen some spectacular entrances at some business conferences – as a clown, on a horse, in a sports car and wheeled in on a bed. People always remember the stunt, but they must also be able to recall its point!

■ I personally find it irritating when people use PowerPoint slides and monotonously reveal bullet point after bullet point, working down a long list. Just because the programme enables you to do this it does not mean you have to. Many slides are also too complicated. Each one should be a highly condensed version of what the presenter might say. Far too many slides look like scripts. I reckon, as a guide, slides should have no more than six bullet points and each point should be a maximum of ten words.

■ The style and tone of voice during delivery has impact too. Serious subjects obviously require a certain formality, but events like farewells must be much lighter in tone. Varying the tone and pitch of your voice will ensure people listen.

■ Nothing irritates me more than when I hear a politician repeat, time after time, the same message as though I am an idiot. It happens all the time and for me it is a big switch-off. However, although it could be seen as 'brainwashing' I have to accept that it works. Look how often US President Barack Obama repeated his mantra 'time for change' in his election campaign. Was that brainwashing?

■ If you happen to be a bit unsure of your delivery, then perhaps a dry run in front of a trusted associate or partner might help.

■ Do you use notes or not? I once worked as speechwriter for General Wolfgang Altenburg, who was Chairman of NATO's Military

Committee and ex-Chief of Defence of Germany. When I first arrived in his employ I would studiously prepare speaking notes for him. A few weeks into my job, when we were going to a meeting where he was due to speak, I noticed he had forgotten his notes. I rushed after him and gave them to him. He half-turned to me as I did so and, pointing with his finger at his forehead, told me he needed 'this' far more than notes to speak. Since that day I have never used a note for speaking. It works for me. But that depends on the individual. Winston Churchill's greatest speeches were always worked out on paper in front of him and normally they were well rehearsed too.

THE POINT OF SPEECHES

I have mentioned that many people have difficulty remembering much of what is said by even the greatest speakers in the world. However, it is still a good form of communication. First, it allows everyone listening to see and hear a leader in person and that direct connection matters to human beings. Second, it gives the leader a chance to put over his or her approach, feelings and character.

British politicians lay great stress on the speeches they make at party political conferences because it is on such occasions that their parties feel they can really get to know their leaders. Of course this is bunkum, as their speeches are largely spin and acting. But political leaders are often judged, probably quite unfairly, on the quality of their conference performance. For this reason they all want to deliver a great speech. The same is true for business leaders at significant company meetings.

VISITS

I used to hate the fandango of formal visits in the Army. Inevitably they meant a huge amount of effort being put into cleaning up and sometimes painting wherever the visit route went. On one royal visit I remember we even had to build a one-time-only flushing lavatory, which was dismantled thereafter. Then there were the rehearsals and repeat rehearsals of presentations, not to mention the dress rehearsal for the visit. I recall one occasion when we had to rehearse a cocktail party for Prince Charles where a stand-in Prince of Wales circulated between groups who were asked to practise their royal small talk. Surely VIPs don't think they get a true feel for the people and place they are visiting on such occasions?

For me, and for so many others, the best way to visit is informally
– by just dropping in to see someone. As commanding officer and as
a managing director I used to allocate at least a portion of the day
to simply turning up and wandering around. The whole business is
user-friendly and real opinions and facts are far more likely to be
forthcoming in consequence. When I was doing the rounds I would
frequently ask what most worried anyone with whom I talked. Under
such circumstances I was far more likely to get a truthful answer than
something manufactured and massaged by an intermediary.

SURVEYS AND SUGGESTIONS

If everything seems perfect then it probably isn't. Sensible leaders
should not get carried away when someone suggests they are brilliant
or an expert. If everyone in an organization thinks all is going swim-
mingly well it may be time for some serious analysis. Complacency is
the sworn enemy of progress, and self-satisfaction can lead to disaster,
especially against a competent enemy on the battlefield or in highly
competitive markets.

I remember a story I heard about a very capable company chairman.
Apparently at one board meeting he looked at an agenda point and
noted that everyone was in agreement on the matter. 'If that is the case
then I will put it back to our next meeting in the hope that we can get
enough disagreement to discuss the point properly,' he declared.

Getting a feel for how an organization thinks collectively can be
achieved relatively easily by surveys or departmental focus groups.
Suggestion boxes have their place, too. Asking every employee to
fill out a questionnaire with specifically designed questions is also a
good technique. But one board of directors for whom I worked, considered the key findings of their own survey to be misplaced and in-
comprehensible. They simply refused to believe what was reported.
That company folded six months later for various reasons, but one of
them was the huge gulf of misunderstanding between management and
staff.

I find it interesting when organizations opt for anonymous surveys.
That worries me a little, even though I understand the good reasons for
it. I think my worry is why company leaders feel they will not get the
truth without this condition. Surely if company employees feel valued
and secure they will also believe that any constructive comments they
make will not be misinterpreted and possibly threaten their positions
or jobs?

PERIODIC NOTICES

In the Army every battalion and each company within them produces their own daily review of what has happened and what is to occur in the immediate future. The battalion level version is called 'Part 1 Orders' and companies call their version 'Company Detail'. The companies wait until daily Part 1 Orders are produced and then write versions directed specifically at their own soldiers. Failure to read and comply with an instruction written on either Part 1 Orders or Company Detail is a chargeable offence so it is a normal part of routine for everyone to read them. By this means all ranks in a military organization get to know what is happening. It is a system almost as old as the British Army and it works well.

I tried a version of this when I was a managing director. Into my civilian version of Part 1 Orders I put future events and visits, programmes for visits to the company, sales targets, and information on our products, movements of key staff and anything else I thought should be known by everyone. The system worked reasonably well but I found we were simply not big enough to produce a daily version and so ended up with one production a week.

Many bigger organizations go for much grander versions. A staff newspaper is a perfectly normal venture in all the largest companies. The big advantage is that everything in these publications is supportive of the top leadership and they are a good, guaranteed place for company leaders to explain what is happening. The disadvantage is that a lot of employees just don't bother to read them because the newsletters are so on-message.

E-MAIL

The internet is a blessing and hugely beneficial to the business community at large. I wonder if the same is quite the case with e-mail. How many times do I hear people complain about the number of e-mails they get daily? Maybe they are a little proud of it too. But, in truth, there is far too much e-mail sloshing around internally in most companies. Some business leaders simply don't open them, or get their personal assistant to vet which ones get through to them. I have even known some rather upfront bosses send e-mails back to the originator with a comment like, 'You are wasting my time. Please don't do it again.' That is a fairly effective way of stopping a serial e-mailer.

I gather that Justin King, Chief Executive of Sainsbury's, banned all e-mails on Wednesdays in a bid to encourage one-to-one communications. Maybe that measure could be extended further. After all, there is no better way to communicate than sitting opposite someone and debating what should be done.

MORTAR ATTACK

I mention earlier that actions can also be an essential part of communication. Such was the case when our base at Vitez in Bosnia was mortared. In early November 1992 a mortar round landed amongst the tents within my base. Luckily nobody was hurt but we had very little idea of who fired the round. Obviously I had to do something about it. A mortar is 'lobbed' through the air and its maximum range is about 5,500 metres. I needed to know where that mortar had come from, and quickly, so that I could take action to stop it happening again.

We scoured the area within a 5,500 metre radius to identify possible culprits. Within that circumference the patrols located three mortar team positions; one manned by Bosnian Muslims and the others by Bosnian Croats. We visited each in turn. All denied attacking us. We told them clearly that if they fired at our camp again we would take punitive action. What each mortar team did not know was that a few hours later, after dark, a standing reconnaissance patrol was hidden close to each of their positions. The patrols reported by radio when the teams they were watching fired.

A few days later another mortar bomb landed on my base. Again by amazing luck nobody was hurt. But one of my standing patrols had seen which mortar fired. It was one of the Bosnian Croat positions.

We took immediate action. We destroyed the mortar base plate quite simply and effectively by driving a Warrior over the offending mortar tube. The tube was totally ruined by the weight of armour. Shortly thereafter I had a short conversation with the local Bosnian Croat commander stressing that he had been warned not to fire at us, but he had done so. I told him one of my standing patrols, positioned very near his mortars, had observed the firing. He was utterly shocked – and maybe a little impressed!

I had used military power rather than military force and it had been effective. Significantly, I had avoided the need to apply rules of engagement because I hadn't opened fire. There was no need for me to even report the action. Most important of all, I had done what I said

I would do and given a clear message – 'We mean what we say. Don't do it again'. The base was never mortared again, by any side in the conflict. We had communicated very effectively by what we did, and our actions spoke louder than words.

THE ULTIMATE COMMUNICATOR

Winston Churchill was a master of the English language and used it to communicate with tremendous effect. On 4 June 1940 Churchill spoke to the House of Commons:

> We shall go on to the end. We shall fight in France, we shall fight on the sea and oceans, we shall fight with growing confidence and growing strength in the air, we shall defend our island, whatever the cost may be. We shall fight on beaches, we shall fight on the landing grounds, we shall fight in the fields and in the streets, we shall fight in the hills; we shall never surrender.

I suspect most people recognize those words, which resounded round the world. They were exactly the right words for the occasion. The context, the place, the time, the audience – all matter when communicating. Communication is a multi-faceted skill that involves far more than just stringing words together. Without it good leaders probably could not exist.

14

Crisis management

THE JOLT OF CRISIS

Everyone understands that crises happen, and normally they arrive out of a clear blue sky. Usually they are unforeseen, sudden and almost always need swift reaction. In contingency planning it makes great sense to remember Murphy's Law; anything that can go wrong, will go wrong.

I very much enjoy the story, possibly apocryphal, of what happened immediately after an American B-29 bomber crashed into the 79th floor of the Empire State Building on 28 July 1945. Two military officers apparently turned up soon afterwards. The junior officer asked his senior, 'What shall we tell the press?' The senior officer replied, 'Deny everything.'

It is vital that leaders quickly get a hold on what is happening then take whatever actions are necessary to mitigate potential disaster. The way a leader behaves in a crisis is hugely influential. Signs of fear, indecision, uncertainty and the like are like contagious diseases and they will spread quickly throughout an organization. In contrast, courage, decisiveness and determination can keep matters under control and in proportion. Silence in a crisis is not golden – it can be very destructive. Leaders need to communicate very quickly their thoughts on the nature of the crisis and what they think must happen to counteract it.

Initial shock and surprise must therefore be replaced by quick thinking, planning, briefing and action. Having taken some initial steps to

Analysis of problem	Initial briefings	Consultation	Plan full response	Brief plan	Action

Figure 14.1 Steps to take in a crisis

deal with a problem, it will require continued and detailed management. Whatever the first plan may be, it will almost certainly require adaptation. Logical steps in responding to a crisis might be illustrated as in Figure 14.1.

A KIDNAPPING IN BOSNIA

During the early afternoon of 15 April 1993 I was visiting Travnik, some 7 miles from my headquarters. I intended to meet with the Bosnian Muslim commander there. But just as I was reaching his headquarters I received a radio message. A senior Bosnian Croat officer named Zivko Totic had been kidnapped in the town of Zenica. During the kidnapping five people had been killed – two of Totic's bodyguards, his driver, his brother-in-law and a passer-by. Totic had disappeared, presumably taken by his assailants. The kidnappers were unknown but were presumed to be Bosnian Muslim supporters.

I immediately realized this was a major crisis, and I had to make it my top priority. If Totic was not recovered quickly, the very tricky and uneasy alliance between the Bosnian Croats and Bosnian Muslims would be ruptured. Open warfare was already on the brink of erupting and this would probably be the straw that broke the camel's back.

The ECMM ambassador, Jean-Pierre Thebault, had called a meeting for 4 pm at the International Hotel in Zenica. He sent a message asking that I join him as soon as possible. It took me a while to get there. I was an hour late and clearly, when I arrived, the meeting was not going well.

Like me the ambassador felt that Totic's kidnapping was likely to be the catalyst that turned the long-simmering conflict between Bosnian Croats and Bosnian Muslims into outright war. My intelligence officer suggested that a mujahideen unit, working with the Bosnian Muslim forces but not for them, might have been responsible. There were several of these foreign units around and they seemed to be a law unto themselves. Soldiers on patrol who had come across them reported that they openly boasted their main aim was to ferment disorder. They proudly proclaimed they worked for nobody but God. As I sat in the toxic atmosphere of the meeting I scribbled a mission analysis in my Filofax.

The meeting ended inconclusively at around 6 pm with the Bosnian Muslim representative, Dzemal Merdan, who I knew, saying he would try and locate Totic. But, to Bosnian Croat anger and dismay, he also added that recovering him would be very difficult.

I always liked and respected Merdan so afterwards I sought him out. He told me that a mujahideen unit had definitely taken Totic to stir up trouble and then he said that they were finding mujahideen units very difficult to control. Apparently this one had just turned up and started operating without any real reference to Bosnian Muslim forces. That was our impression too. After Merdan confirmed what we thought already I knew that getting Totic back would be near-impossible. We did not have long to wait for a reaction.

Very early the next morning Bosnian Croat forces attacked the Bosnian Muslims in force right across central Bosnia. Massacres began simultaneously – particularly along the River Lasva valley, where large numbers of civilians were murdered. The crisis was to last for three weeks and from the start its resolution became my top priority. The kidnapping of Totic was a disaster, though what had happened to him was sidelined by the subsequent brutality of communities setting on one another.

MILITARY CRISIS TEAM

My core crisis team was permanently established in Bosnia and consisted of my second in command, the operations officer, the regimental sergeant major and the public relations officer. To these were added others, such as company commanders, the intelligence officer, civil military coordination officers and the quartermaster, when the need arose. During the Lasva Valley fighting we also established a joint Army–European Community Monitoring Mission (ECMM) team. It was led by Jeremy Fleming, a brave ECMM official. Jeremy and I decided that his team must also include representatives from the two warring factions and we managed to get the deputy commanders of both the Bosnian Croats and Bosnian Muslims as members. That was really important. Led by Jeremy the team acted like firefighters, rushing

Figure 14.2 Second Lieutenant Tudor Ellis negotiates on the front lines in Gornji Vakuf

around the region trying to stop conflict wherever it was happening. It was a highly dangerous activity for all involved.

For my part I spent all my time organizing patrols and visiting various local commanders trying to get them to stop fighting. In between such visits I chaired ceasefire meetings – one after the other. It was also vital for me to report what was happening to UN Headquarters in Sarajevo, and for that matter down the national chain of command as well. It was an exhausting period that lasted some three weeks before the region calmed down. But the crisis had cost a lot – well over a hundred people, mainly civilians, had been killed by its conclusion.

IMMEDIATE ACTIONS IN A CRISIS

Just like in the kidnapping of Totic, any business crisis requires immediate, dynamic action. Delay will probably make matters worse – perhaps considerably so. The crucial first action is to understand exactly what has happened and what needs to be put right. Whoever leads needs to get up to speed on the problem very quickly. Maximum effort must be put into establishing accurate facts as first reports are often very inaccurate.

If there isn't a crisis team one must be appointed immediately and it should normally include the chief executive or someone very close to him or her. At its first meeting that team should establish what has happened and take whatever decisions require immediate attention. Crisis team members should be allocated specific tasks and a timeline to achieve them. Normally each person will report on his or her responsibilities at every meeting so that the entire team is continually updated. A set agenda might also help. It can be very simple, covering what is happening, particular problems, options, decisions to be taken, tasks, time of next meeting and any other business.

For any leader the best way of knowing what has happened is to get to the problem area and assess matters personally. In December 1982, when I lost six soldiers and had over thirty others wounded in the Ballykelly bomb, Mrs Thatcher, as Prime Minister, visited us within days. She told me she wanted to assess exactly what had happened and what was needed to avoid a repetition of the disaster.

THE CRISIS MANAGEMENT TEAM

Many companies have a crisis team in readiness or at least pre-assigned. Industry sometimes calls them tiger teams. Ideally they should be small. Maybe four or five people at a maximum unless there are good reasons for having more. They are centres for action and decisions, certainly not committees for long debate. Above all they must have the power to act.

In crises small response teams make obvious sense. During the First World War, Prime Minister Lloyd George appointed a war cabinet of just four people including himself. He was reacting to the inertia shown by the previous Asquith war cabinet, which was huge and quite unable to make timely decisions. Lloyd George's war cabinet included Winston Churchill. It was lean, effective, able to assemble quickly and made rapid decisions. Soon Lloyd George's team brought its influence to bear on key issues such as recruitment, shipping, food supply and the manufacturing of munitions.

When it came to his turn as Prime Minister, Winston Churchill was undoubtedly influenced by his experiences in the previous war. Churchill's war cabinet from May 1940–May 1945 consisted of between six to eight ministers at most and sometimes far fewer than that.

During the 1982 Falklands War Prime Minister Margaret Thatcher appointed a war cabinet of just four people including herself. In 2001 Tony Blair had a war cabinet of eight ministers. The common feature of these war cabinets is that members were selected on the basis of what an individual could contribute to the enterprise, rather than because of the position they held. It's a good point to note.

A business crisis team should have real decision-making power that can commit the company to an action. It must include people of power and influence, probably including the chief executive. Its mission is simple; to comprehend, contain and then fix the crisis. Communications must be managed and normal day-to-day business is likely to be ongoing too. Some in the crisis team may have to spend all their time on that task and therefore might have to be relieved of all other duties.

One benefit from crises is the experience it gives to those who have taken part. Calm seas do not make great sailors. People who have weathered a crisis are normally the better for it. Their confidence grows, and with it their usefulness to any organization. Someone who has been under fire and coped with it is far better than a virgin soldier. Crises are great training grounds. In business someone who has dealt with a real problem and has been instrumental in finding a solution probably feels much more on top of the job as a result.

THE SPOKESPERSON

Any crisis team's initial meeting must start by determining exactly what has happened and what needs to be put right. Its next decision is probably who should be its spokesperson. Someone in the company has to say what has happened as quickly as possible. Moreover, that story should not be 'spun' to appear in a good light. It is crucial that the company spokesperson tells the truth.

The spokesperson should be a member of the crisis team, or at least attend its meetings. They should also be available at any time of the day and night or, if that is not possible, proper alternative arrangements should be made. Ideally a spokesperson should be someone known and trusted by the media and as many other audiences as possible. The integrity of the spokesperson should be beyond reproach and he or she should never be put in any position that might bring this into doubt.

By the end of my time in Bosnia I had several spokespersons. They were in constant contact with the media and also became a conduit between correspondents and me. Each night they attended my daily meetings; they organized press conferences, briefings and face-to-face meetings, and generally tried to help journalists do their job. They were liked and trusted, which was essential to their success.

Any spokesperson should:

- be available quickly and accessible to the media;
- build up a rapport and keep credibility with journalists;
- have the ability to make informed, accurate and careful comments on or off the record;
- develop a reputation for decency and honesty;
- be publicly known as on or close to the crisis team.

Communication must work both internally and externally. Company staff should also know what is happening because they have that right and because each and every one of them is a spokesperson for the company when they talk to family and friends or if they are approached by reporters.

A company that refuses to talk to the media or states 'no comment' invites unhelpful speculation. Such actions can suggest there is something suspicious about what has happened, or indeed that something is wrong. In Bosnia my spokesman was straight: 'I'm sorry but I don't know' or 'I'm not allowed to say any more for security reasons' was normally accepted. Its civilian equivalent 'I'm afraid I have no more information at the moment but will get it as soon as possible' is also a much better way of saying 'No comment'.

STATEMENTS AND THE TRUTH

When an Army patrol on operations encounters the enemy it sends a contact report over the radio. It consisting of five elements

AT: Time and date.
AT: Location and what has happened.
WHAT: You are doing about it now.
WHAT: You want to do about it in future.
WHAT: You feel about the situation – apology even if not to blame!

Such a template could be very useful to structure a company crisis statement.

The truth will come out. If it is distorted or significant facts are conveniently forgotten they will emerge at some stage, often at the worst time. In one case of product contamination that I advised on, the company refused to say what had really happened for far too long. Eventually it was forced to admit its mistake, and its credibility with consumers took an even greater hit than it might have done if it had been honest from the start.

Too often there is a real conflict between ethics and legal advice. Despite the fact that a company may have made a pretty drastic mistake, its legal advisers frequently suggest that a simple admittance of error is not appropriate. Such lawyers are not crooks but are simply doing their job, trying to avoid the possibility of any potentially expensive compensation claims. This is a fine line, which involves careful thought. Telling the truth is best, but admitting liability can be very costly too. The crisis team will have to spend time on this, tailoring its words carefully. Obviously, legal officers in companies should also be either in a crisis team or at least be part of its decision cycle.

AUDIENCES

Unless someone puts a well thought-through response to the crisis, the press is likely to make its own mind up about what has happened, and it may not be to your liking, or in line with the true facts.

As well as the media, other audiences include:

- Employees. They can play a major part in crisis resolution. They are likely to be approached directly by the media and need to know exactly what is happening. They have a vested interest in the company and will be naturally worried about their own future. Of course, if redundancies are likely, employees should know about them as soon as possible.
- Consumers. It is normal for consumers to distrust companies in crises. Consumers worry for themselves and their families. Addressing this matter quickly is a top priority. The speed of business recovery after a crisis may well be determined entirely by consumer attitudes.
- Dependent businesses. Franchisees, retail outlets and distributors must also feature in crisis plans. When a major company is in crisis so too are all those smaller organizations that depend on it. They too are likely to lose money or be sued for non-delivery of goods

or services, and their survival may be directly linked to the way the crisis is handled.

- The investment community. This is obviously an important audience. Analysts, the media and banks have a vital influence on institutional and individual investors. The investment community wants to know the truth about what has happened. They need to be convinced that the crisis will be resolved – preferably very quickly. If this audience feels that the crisis is being well handled and it is under control their influence will be crucial in the battle to preserve share value. The reverse is equally true.
- The local community. Nobody should ignore how a local community feels. They matter, especially if many of them are employees and likely to lose their jobs. There may well be anger at potential jobs lost, and environmental or other damage. Local communities normally have the ear of local politicians, particularly if the media highlights local reactions such as public meetings and protest marches.
- Politicians and local authorities. These people will inevitably have an interest in what is happening – particularly if regulations or health matters are an issue. Some politicians, national as well as local, have been known to see crises as an opportunity for their own personal advancement. Beware the politician who seeks the main chance at your expense!
- Experts. Society now has an increasing plethora of so-called experts. Such people are always available for comment. Often they have far more credibility than anyone else because the public feel they have no particular axe to grind. They too should be kept on side.

If you are a member of a crisis team it is terribly important that you try to stay objective in both reasoning and behaviour. A key test might be to ask whether you would believe what the team is about to state publicly – if, of course, you didn't happen to be so crucially involved. Key messages must reflect the truth and are likely to include:

- You care greatly and apologize if at fault.
- You have everything under control.
- You are taking effective action.
- You are honest and will deal with mistakes openly and fairly.
- You are doing your best.
- You are working with all the appropriate authorities – particularly on safety.

CONTINGENCY PLANS

It is just not possible to anticipate or pre-empt all problems, but that should not stop contingency plans being made – even if only in a generic format. Such preliminary organization for potential disasters makes great sense. Let me give a few obvious examples. For food manufacturers it is crucial to set up plans to deal with product contamination – either accidental or deliberate. I have worked with some shipping companies where sensible contingency planning scenarios always involve ships sinking or going aground. Then, for an energy company, I worked out what they might do when disasters like fires or explosions happen aboard their ships, in their facilities or in their fuel transporters. In truth all commercial enterprises should think through 'What if?' scenarios.

Normal outline contingency crisis plans include some or all of the following:

- potential disaster scenario;
- aim;
- outline plan;
- tasks allotted;
- top level support for decision makers;
- funding;
- responsibilities;
- crisis command centre location and organization;
- communication with staff and all audiences.

The MoD probably has more contingency plans than any other government department. Those that deal with foreign situations are called Joint Theatre Plans (JTPs). A huge number of JTPs have been written to anticipate what are called services-assisted evacuations. It may surprise some, but the MoD has plans to get British nationals out of almost every country in the world should circumstances require it. I wrote a few of them myself when I was serving in the MoD's military operations branch. Not only are these JTPs regularly reviewed by the staff officers who would implement them but they are also sometimes rehearsed on exercises too. Some commercial companies follow similar practices. I have taken part in a few commercial crisis exercises, normally to practise emergency actions after I had helped design them.

Rehearsing what might happen in crises is invaluable for two reasons. First, it allows leaders to assess whether the plans they have designed really work and are practical. Second, it helps those involved in a real crisis later to be much more confident in the way they handle it. But, in truth, even the best-prepared contingency crisis plans are unlikely to cover exactly what might happen. Life is always full of surprises.

Let me give just one example of contingency planning which is often overlooked. It involves telephones. A well-prepared company should maintain a series of inactive phone lines, unused but ready for action. But there is more to it than just that. For example, in crises emergency telephones will require manning – perhaps for 24 hours a day. Who should do that? Then every incoming call has also to be properly logged and, if necessary, appropriate action taken. Who will do that, and what about training for the task?

ACCEPTING RESPONSIBILITY

A few weeks after the successful landings on D Day (6 June 1944) General Eisenhower, the Supreme Allied Commander, apparently found a forgotten note in his pocket. It was a holding statement in the event of Allied failure on the beaches of Normandy:

> Our landings in the Cherbourg-Havre area have failed to gain a satisfactory foothold and I have withdrawn the troops. My decision to attack at this time and place was based on the best information available. The troops, the air force and navy, did all that bravery and devotion to duty could do. If any blame or fault attaches to the attempt it is mine alone.

Given the risk of failure on D Day, which seemed a huge gamble at the time, Eisenhower showed true leadership. He had his contingency statement for failure ready – just in case. He hoped for the best but made a contingency plan for the worst. If things had gone wrong it was he who would have taken responsibility. It may not have been his fault, yet he knew, as the commander, he would be responsible and accepted it.

Of course leaders shouldn't sidestep their responsibilities for mistakes or failure. I remember listening to Sir Richard Branson on BBC Radio Five Live when there had been a big mistake involving Virgin Trains. Actually it was largely the fault of the line operating company, Railtrack.

But that didn't matter a jot to customers and Branson knew it. Asked to account for what had happened he replied:

> We messed up. It was completely our fault. I take full responsibility for it. We're obviously looking at not doing it again in the future but there's no point in hiding from the fact that we've got to do this better in the future if we are to make this business work.

Branson then took further positive steps to correct the mistakes made and, as a result, he defused a highly damaging incident. Yet for some leaders the hardest thing is to apologize. It shouldn't be so. A simple, uncomplicated apology can be very effective – as well as the right thing to do.

15

Reflections

LEADING IS UNIVERSAL

The best leaders have 'fire in their bellies'. They want to lead. Such a desire is straightforward and honest. Most also love the thrill of leading. It can give a zest for life and can become all-consuming.

I have highlighted some great leaders who have seized their moment, inspired countless people, and sometimes changed human history. Leaders like Napoleon and Churchill are 'superheroes', to use modern vernacular. There are libraries full of their exploits and sayings, and many films have been made about them. But leadership isn't just confined to these very special people. It is universal, normal and quite ordinary too.

Some children lead other children. Parents lead their children. Teachers lead their classes. Priests lead their congregations. Editors lead their journalists. Chefs lead their cooks. Officers lead their soldiers. Business executives lead their employees. So it goes on. Leading in its basic form is the ability to show the way and guide others to achieve something. Most people don't even understand they are leading because it comes so naturally – they do it instinctively. Everyone is a leader at some stage, in one form or other and often without even realizing it.

PASSION

Like a contagious disease, passion is catching. It is the vital drive that fuels really effective leadership. Passion is directly connected to strength of conviction. Leaders have a responsibility to provide conviction and a firm opinion on what needs to be done. I cannot think of any good leaders who do not exhibit some passion.

Leaders who show little commitment, enthusiasm or passion are unlikely to have a loyal or sizeable following. A dour, unenthusiastic, dispassionate and unresponsive demeanour is not usually the best way to inspire others. However, we humans are funny creatures and I have met some such people in positions of leadership. One Army general I knew had a brilliant brain and was a hugely accomplished tactician but he was taciturn, severe and very dull company. Yet he must have had a sense of humour. At one dinner party at the Army staff college an officer's wife sat next to him. He said nothing and just stared into space. Eventually the officer's wife said, 'You know I have been bet ten pounds that I can get you to say three words to me during dinner.' The general looked at her without any warmth, said 'You lost', and didn't speak to her again during the meal.

DETERMINATION AND SELF-BELIEF

Leaders should of course be determined to win or succeed. They should also have an inner self-belief that they can do it. Leaders make things happen. They may have some doubts; I had plenty in my career. But these must have no effect on their determination to succeed. In just the same way as courage is the overcoming of fear, so true leadership involves the subjugation of self-doubt. The best leaders never see a bottle as half-empty – it is half-full, but only temporarily as they are going to fill it.

Leadership is all about resolve and self-assurance that you are right. It is not for anyone who is afraid to make a decision in case it goes against them. A lot of decisions are likely to be wrong. That's life! A leader has to risk making mistakes and then put them right fast when they occur.

EMOTION

Leaders often have short tempers – especially when they feel they have been let down. Emotion is a tool a leader can use to devastating effect, provided it is not overdone. Certain leaders may rant and swear, but a person whose rages are predictable or permanent soon loses effect. Temper can be very effective in suddenly getting the team to shift up a gear or two. But it cannot be contrived, forecast or continuous as it rapidly loses effect. It is very difficult to be logical when in a temper. A continuously angry leader will also have difficulty communicating with others.

Emotion should be spontaneous and heartfelt. During his time as Prime Minister, Winston Churchill visited the East End of London after a particularly vicious German air raid. As he was going around the bombsites a woman saw tears in his eyes. 'Look,' she declared, 'he really cares.' Churchill himself owned up to being 'a bit of a blubber' but it had its effect.

In public speaking emotion can convert a mediocre performance into a great one. As human beings we spend our lives communicating with one another in a variety of ways. Many, if not most, of us have become fairly expert at determining someone's sincerity just by watching and listening to them, and most people are pretty good at identifying when people are insincere.

Today's political leaders get very nervous and psyched up about big speeches. They fully understand that every nuance of language and physical gesture will be analysed. Above all they want to appear to be sincere, as they realize how important this is. That is why keynote addresses are rehearsed ad nauseam and carefully stage-managed.

On 26 September 1960 John F Kennedy and Richard Nixon took part in the first televised US presidential election debate ever. This gave American voters a real opportunity to see their candidates in competition, and the contrast was stark. Nixon had seriously injured his knee the month before, and had spent two weeks in hospital. By the time of the first debate he was still 20 pounds underweight and he had a deathly pallor. He arrived at the TV studio in an ill-fitting shirt, and refused make-up to improve his colour and lighten his perpetual '5 o'clock shadow'. Kennedy, by contrast, had spent early September campaigning in California. He was tanned, confident and well rested. Even Nixon noted the contrast. 'I had never seen him looking so fit,' he wrote later. Looks hardly helped Nixon but his manner of speaking set the seal on his fate. Whereas Kennedy gave the impression of being open and very human, Nixon's performance suggested he was the reverse and his nickname of 'Tricky Dicky' seemed confirmed.

A speech or address given without emotion may have its place, but it is usually inappropriate for those who seek to lead. Leaders make speeches to inform, inspire or both – no truly great address by any leader has been devoid of emotion.

ROBUSTNESS

Real leaders just keep going. They don't give up. Robustness is always required, especially under pressure. General Montgomery met his match with Winston Churchill just after he had been appointed to command the 8th Army. Montgomery boasted to Churchill: 'I don't smoke, I don't drink, and I am 100 per cent fit.' Churchill replied, 'I both smoke and drink, and I am 200 per cent fit.' He certainly had great stamina for a man who was almost 70 years old at the time.

In truth Churchill must have been incredibly robust, existing on very little sleep and taking even that in catnaps. During the Blitz, newsreels captured the energy of his wartime leadership. He was shown visiting factories, shipyards, and cities demolished by German bombs. Scurrying along, he seemed to be in a constant hurry. He perpetually carried walking sticks, used to point and prod dynamically rather than as supports. All the time he held or chewed a cigar, which often lasted for hours. As he pushed on he flashed his famous 'V for victory' signs. Churchill's potent spirit of perseverance and determination is best summed up in one of his own maxims: 'We must just KBO.' The initials stood for 'Keep Buggering On'.

KNOWING THE ORGANIZATION

When top leaders ask questions they do not necessarily get truthful answers. In big organizations responses are commonly filtered and massaged up through various levels, which often leads to a greatly watered-down effect. When I worked in the MoD as a desk officer and thus an original drafter of papers I noticed that time and time again the final document that went to the Army board was nothing like the one I had originally drafted. Its recommendations were often changed beyond recognition. Obviously as such papers ascend the chain of responsibility other factors come into play, but far too often I felt that the content was changed simply so as not to upset the 'top brass'.

I recall one excellent senior officer in the MoD who was fully aware of this phenomenon. Refreshingly, he started to ask for a brief on the differences between the originally drafted paper and the final version. The first of such briefs made very interesting reading. But then the MoD adjusted itself to deal with his impudence. Shortly thereafter all original draft papers had to be semi-approved up the chain before their first circulation. The system sorted it in the end.

Even if the 'truth' does get through to top executives it might not have much impact. Sometimes company surveys highlight problems very well but their findings do not fit preconceptions and are ignored by board members. When given the results of surveys that conflict with their established views far too many executives simply bury them. They do so at their peril.

Of course, leaders should know what they are doing. Really that goes without saying. Most successful entrepreneurs start their businesses themselves, doing everything and knowing the businesses inside out. In the Army it's not the quite the same because officers join an organization that has been functioning for hundreds of years. Commanding officers master their trade as they progress through the ranks of second lieutenant, lieutenant, captain and major, commanding at all those levels before assuming their appointments. There is some similarity, though, as both entrepreneurs and Army officers should be well grounded by experience in their respective enterprises.

LUCK

Being ready to go when that lucky opportunity presents itself is crucial. I was fortunate to be commanding a battalion that was relatively free of commitments just at the time when the British Government decided to send troops into the Balkans. Napoleon always asked if officers he was about to promote were lucky. Maybe luck can be given a helping hand. Brent Hoberman, one of the two founders of lastminute.com, believes so – 'Most entrepreneurs will say they have been lucky. But you also have to create opportunities to be lucky.'

How, then, might people improve their own luck? That is a difficult one but there might be some ways to perk up destiny. Here are some ideas that seem to have helped Richard Branson and James Dyson make their own luck:

- Acceptance of responsibility. They accept that they are responsible for what occurs in and to their organization and blame nobody else if things go wrong. When there was a big mistake involving Virgin Trains Branson went public on Radio 5 Live and stated that he fully accepted responsibility for what had happened.
- Learning from mistakes. They learn from their errors. Both Branson and Dyson have publicly stated that they made lots of mistakes. The trick seems to have been that they learnt from the errors and didn't repeat them.
- Perseverance. They don't give up or put off decisions, and if a problem occurs they act to sort it out quickly.
- Risk taking. They are prepared to run risks to advance their businesses. Dyson encourages his employees to try new approaches and agrees that they will fail more often than not.
- Confidence. They have confidence in themselves, their staff and their organizations. Branson was confident enough to go head-to-head with established transatlantic airlines and even to set up Virgin Rail when his chances of making a success of rail travel were deemed to be very slight indeed.

RESPONSIBILITY

It has sometimes been my terribly sad duty to speak with the families of soldiers who have been killed under my command. It was very difficult, as I felt deeply wretched and utterly responsible for the deaths of their loved ones. Amazingly the families almost invariably gently rebuked me for blaming myself. They normally said I was wrong and was not at fault. But I wasn't wrong, for if I was not responsible for what happened to soldiers under my command then who was?

Many people try to evade their responsibilities when things go pearshaped. If something goes wrong they might even appear on television, radio or in newspapers blaming the system, external forces, other people or indeed anything or anyone but themselves. Watching such wriggling is often pretty nauseating. If the wrigglers survive in their jobs, they will have lost not just prestige but also a great deal of loyalty from superiors and subordinates alike.

DECISION TAKING

Leaders take decisions. Easy ones are just that, but what defines a leader is the ability to take the tough ones. Hopefully most decisions will be right, but they are likely to be wrong quite often too. I have never blamed officers who made mistakes or poor decisions unless it became a trend. In my view there is one crime greater than continually making wrong decisions, and that is the failure to make any at all.

I once heard an officer being decried, not because he made bad decisions but because he wouldn't ever make one. Everyone called him 'Noddy' because he simply nodded all the time when being briefed. The nodding didn't mean he agreed – it was simply a mannerism and, if anything, it meant 'I don't know what to do.' He should never have passed officer selection. It is better to take a decision that might need revision than to muddle along indecisively. Good leaders also have the strength to accept a mistake and make amends.

RISK TAKING

The reason why some people cannot take a decision is because they are risk averse. To act is to risk, and good leaders just get on with it. Doing things the same way as they have always been done reduces risk, but stultifies progress. In business most entrepreneurs are risk takers. If they get it right they reap the rewards, but novelty is chancy. Most entrepreneurs fail and fail again before finally making their breakthrough. This was certainly the case with Dyson, who developed over 5,000 prototypes before he could get his revolutionary vacuum cleaner into the market. He feely admits that half of his business decisions to date have been wrong. Yet he still encourages all on his team to take risks, make mistakes and try doing what nobody else has done before. Dyson has a very clear understanding of the role of mistakes in business; 'Enjoy failure and learn from it. You can never learn from success.'

Admiral 'Titch' Cowan, Commander British Naval Forces in the Baltic in 1919, valued the idea of risk extremely highly: 'Nothing is worthwhile unless there's a risk in it. Always choose the boldest course if you have any choice at all; it is always the boldest course that stands the best chance of success.' I don't wholly agree with this view, but it is certainly a thought-provoking way of looking at life.

TRAPPINGS OF OFFICE

Both military and business promotions bring greater privilege – the trappings of office. Growing responsibilities normally have commensurate rewards that are much more than simply financial. Your own office, a window seat, a company car, a reserved parking place, club class travel and similar perks are enticing inducements to everyone but the most high-minded.

There is always a small danger that such incentives cause barriers to real understanding of what it is like at the sharp end. Generals sitting in châteaux miles behind the front lines in the First World War are an obvious example. But it must also be difficult to understand what is happening on a production line if the nearest you ever get to it is by passing it in your company car as you go to the executive entrance. Those in charge must never forget the real business. There are some (rare) companies who remind their top executives of this by insisting on a 'back to basics' day once a year. Everyone gets an annual reality check by completing a shift where the real business and money is made.

PREJUDICE AND FAVOURITISM

Whoever leads must be free from all prejudice. Sadly race, sex, ethnicity, sexual orientation, age and religion all continue to incite prejudicial behaviour by some members of society and even a few leaders. It is unacceptable for a leader to have any characteristics of intolerance, bigotry, chauvinism or discrimination. In this respect prejudice and favouritism are linked.

I can think of at least one general in the Army (dead now) who most definitely had favourites. He repeatedly advanced them above other equally qualified officers. We knew who the favourites were, indeed they were identified as such by declaring themselves to be members of a group which used the general's nickname. Frankly it was appalling and very poor leadership by the general. Leaders must be fair and even-handed. Favouritism and prejudice are deeply wrong, hugely divisive and weaken anyone's ability to lead.

POPULARITY

Being liked is always pleasant but it may not be necessary for a leader. General Bill Slim was adored by his soldiers but Wellington, Churchill and Montgomery were far less popular. Slim put the welfare of his men as a top priority and drastically reduced malaria, the biggest killer in his 14th Army. Wellington called his men 'the scum of the earth' and meant it. He flogged and hanged them without a second's thought if necessary. Churchill was conceited, irritatingly self-assured and an unreliable friend. People hugely respected him but he wasn't really a warm person. Montgomery was even less likeable as a person. He was also quite prepared to rob credit from his predecessor, General Auchinleck, who had carried out the vast majority of detailed preparations ready for the Battle of El Alamein in 1942. Later on he additionally forgot whose idea (his) failed at Arnhem in 1944 – implying others were to blame.

Unlike politicians, business leaders do not depend on general elections for their power. They are not in a popularity contest. As appointed leaders they have subsequent autocracy. Their decisions should be made for the right reasons and that may not include popularity. If popular decisions determined progress then companies could be led by a continuous voting system amongst employees, perhaps with the executives setting the questions.

Leaders sometimes have to make what some call 'bet your job' decisions where they decide on action that, if matters go wrong, could result in their dismissal. Certainly I can think of at least one such choice I made in Bosnia. It concerned my deliberate decision to blame Bosnian Croat soldiers for the massacre at Ahmici on 22 April 1993. I knew full well that my instructions were to maintain strict neutrality and that such an action at least bent my orders. However, I felt that I could not simply sit on the fence when there was clear evidence of a war crime having been committed and I knew which side was responsible. I realized that several of my superior officers felt I had gone too far, but the Geneva Conventions are clear where an officer's responsibilities lie with regard to crimes against humanity.

People being led want decisions. Surprisingly enough taking tough, sometimes deeply unpopular decisions can occasionally lead to unexpected popularity when they work. Hard choices well made often bring success, and winning leaders normally get more popular. Everyone loves a winner.

FAIRNESS AND HONESTY

Leaders like Wellington, Montgomery, Slim, Leighton, Dyson and Branson all exhibit the important traits of fairness and honesty in their actions. They dealt with their people properly. Nobody ever suggests they were guilty of favouritism – except insofar as certain people might be lauded for their achievements.

Nobody knows you better than you do yourself. You are the very best person to judge your own strengths and weaknesses – provided you are honest about them. When superior officers handed me my annual confidential reports and I read them I knew straight away which of the comments made really hit the mark.

MANNERS AND VISITS

Busy leaders have to ration their time, but they should never under-estimate just how important it is to put aside space for personal visits. It is a signal that those who they visit matter. They matter because the leader spends time with an individual. Such personal contact is so much more powerful than an anonymous 'round robin' letter or e-mail.

Meeting the boss can have a profound effect on how personnel perform. In Bosnia I was informed that the Prince of Wales was to visit on 16 March 1993. At first I thought it would be a distraction we didn't need. I was so wrong. In just a few hours the Prince met or talked with as many soldiers as possible. His visit was terribly popular and he made all who met him feel that they mattered. Prince Charles' time with us was a great fillip to morale.

Remembering and using people's correct names is simple good manners – enough said. What impression is given, though, when a leader doesn't look up or stop working when someone goes into his or her office? The visitor is clearly not a high priority. These days, writing 'thank you' letters and sending them by post takes second place to a quick e-mail. In 2005, when John Major was appointed as a Knight of the Garter, I wrote him a letter of congratulations. He sent me a reply; quite a long, personal one and in his own hand. That mattered; it confirmed my impression of him as a thoroughly decent man and it pleased me. Such a small thing to do but it had a significant impact.

PERSONAL CARE

Everyone in an organization has to be 'fit for purpose'. Leading is mentally and even physically demanding at times. The brain never stops, mental stress can be immense and sometimes the hours of work required put a huge strain on the physique. It is no good being superb at your job but not able to deal with the mental or physical strain of it. I personally am very bad at looking after myself, so these ideas for maintaining physical and mental health most definitely apply to me too:

■ Talk things over with a confidant, such as a partner or friend. Discussing things in a confidential atmosphere might help you work through what is really worrying you.
■ Take a break from the job by going somewhere peaceful where nobody can reach you, and go for long enough that you can stop thinking about the job.

Figure 15.1 Arriving back in Germany with Richard Rochester and Matthew Dundas-Whatley in May 1993

- Encourage constructive criticism and do not take it personally.
- Take regular physical exercise.

FINAL THOUGHTS

There is no magic formula that produces the perfect leader. Leaders are designed by the time, place, circumstances, task, team and individuals involved, their training and probably most of all by their own innate character. Personal honesty, integrity, passion, pride, humility, intelligence and courage are just some of the virtues that determine how individuals lead.

There will always be ways to improve leadership performance. Leadership models are great for inspiration and ideas and I hope my own thoughts on how to lead, developed first in the Army, have some practical benefit to business leaders too. In the final analysis, however, just as no two people are exactly alike, so no two leaders work in the same way and your own personal style will be based to a great extent on your own character and experience.

Whoever you are, and whatever your style of leadership, leading others is a great privilege. Good luck, enjoy the experience, and do your very best for those you are lucky enough to lead.